WIDENING HORIZONS

British judges increasingly now pay attention to foreign case law when deciding domestic cases, and are required to interpret and apply international law in domestic courts and administer an international code of human rights. Tom Bingham examines the consequences of this increasingly internationalist outlook of British courts, including cases which rely on a range of foreign authorities, cases where an international convention or principle is interpreted and cases in which human rights issues are decided in reliance on principles established elsewhere.

LORD THOMAS BINGHAM, Baron Bingham of Cornhill, has held the posts of Master of the Rolls, Lord Chief Justice and Senior Law Lord. He presided over key judgments, including the ruling in the Belmarsh case that it was unlawful, and a breach of human rights, to detain foreign terrorist suspects without charge, and the ruling that evidence against terror suspects obtained by torture was inadmissible.

WIDENING HORIZONS

The Influence of Comparative Law and International Law on Domestic Law

THOMAS H. BINGHAM

CAMBRIDGE
UNIVERSITY PRESS

CAMBRIDGE UNIVERSITY PRESS
Cambridge, New York, Melbourne, Madrid, Cape Town, Singapore,
São Paulo, Delhi, Dubai, Tokyo

Cambridge University Press
The Edinburgh Building, Cambridge CB2 8RU, UK

Published in the United States of America by Cambridge University Press, New York

www.cambridge.org
Information on this title: www.cambridge.org/9780521199353

First published 2010

Printed in the United Kingdom at the University Press, Cambridge

A catalogue record for this publication is available from the British Library

Library of Congress Cataloguing in Publication data
Bingham, T. H. (Thomas Henry), 1933–
  Widening horizons : the influence of comparative law and international law on
  domestic law / Thomas H. Bingham.
    p. cm. – (The Hamlyn lectures)
  Includes bibliographical references and index.
  ISBN 978-0-521-19935-3 – ISBN 978-0-521-13802-4 (pbk.)
  1. International and municipal law–Great Britain. 2. Comparative law–Great
Britain. I. Title. II. Series.
  KD4015.B56 2010
  341′.040941–dc22   2010011223

ISBN 978-0-521-19935-3 Hardback
ISBN 978-0-521-13802-4 Paperback

CONTENTS

The Hamlyn Trust   vi

The Hamlyn Lectures   x

1 'Foreign moods, fads, or fashions'   1

2 'Wider still and wider'   29

3 Nonsense on international stilts?   55

Index   84

v

The Hamlyn Trust owes its existence today to the will of the late Miss Emma Warburton Hamlyn of Torquay, who died in 1941 at the age of 80. She came of an old and well-known Devon family. Her father, William Bussell Hamlyn, practised in Torquay as a solicitor and JP for many years, and it seems likely that Miss Hamlyn founded the trust in his memory. Emma Hamlyn was a woman of strong character, intelligent and cultured, well-versed in literature, music and art, and a lover of her country. She travelled extensively in Europe and Egypt, and apparently took considerable interest in the law and ethnology of the countries and cultures that she visited. An account of Miss Hamlyn by Professor Chantal Stebbings of the University of Exeter (one of the Hamlyn trustees) may be found, under the title 'The Hamlyn Legacy', in volume 42 of the published lectures.

Miss Hamlyn bequeathed the residue of her estate on trust in terms which it seems were her own. The wording was thought to be vague, and the will was taken to the Chancery Division of the High Court, which in November 1948 approved a Scheme for the administration of the trust. Paragraph 3 of the Scheme, which follows Miss Hamlyn's own wording, is as follows:

> The object of the charity is the furtherance by lectures
> or otherwise among the Common People of the United

Kingdom of Great Britain and Northern Ireland of
the knowledge of the Comparative Jurisprudence and
Ethnology of the Chief European countries including the
United Kingdom, and the circumstances of the growth
of such jurisprudence to the Intent that the Common
People of the United Kingdom may realise the privileges
which in law and custom they enjoy in comparison with
other European Peoples and realising and appreciating
such privileges may recognise the responsibilities and
obligations attaching to them.

The Trustees are to include the Vice-Chancellor of the
University of Exeter, representatives of the Universities of
London, Leeds, Glasgow, Belfast and Wales and persons co-
opted. At present there are eight Trustees:

From the outset it was decided that the objects of the Trust
could be best achieved by means of an annual course of public lectures of outstanding interest and quality by eminent

lecturers, and by their subsequent publication and distribution to a wider audience. The first of the Lectures were delivered by the Rt Hon. Lord Justice Denning (as he then was) in 1949. Since then there has been an unbroken series of annual Lectures published until 2005 by Sweet & Maxwell and from 2006 by Cambridge University Press. A complete list of the Lectures may be found on pages x to xiii. In 2005 the Trustees decided to supplement the Lectures with an annual Hamlyn Seminar, normally held at the Institute of Advanced Legal Studies in the University of London, to mark the publication of the Lectures in printed book form. The Trustees have also, from time to time, provided financial support for a variety of projects which, in various ways, have disseminated knowledge or have promoted to a wider public understanding of the law.

This, the 61st, series of lectures was delivered by Lord Bingham in three different locations. The first took place at Newton House, Dinefwr Castle near Llandeilo, South Wales. The second was held at the Museum Lecture Theatre at Cardiff University Law School and the third was held at the Lecture Theatre at the London offices of Clifford Chance in the Docklands. The Board of Trustees would like to record its appreciation to Lord Bingham himself and also the Swansea and Cardiff University law schools, as well as the partners of Clifford Chance who generously hosted these Lectures. Traversing from the west to the east of the country the Lectures moved from a small castle in West Wales, to the Museum of Wales by a Winter Wonderland in Cardiff and onto the Docklands to and from which great ships carried out international

viii

commerce in years gone by. These were all a fitting tribute to the Welsh associations of the Lecturer and to the subject of the lectures – widening the horizons of the law.

December 2009, London
AVROM SHERR
Chairman of the Trustees

1949   Freedom under the Law by the Rt Hon. Lord Denning
1950   The Inheritance of the Common Law by Richard O'Sullivan
1951   The Rational Strength of English Law by Professor F. H. Lawson
1952   English Law and the Moral Law by Professor A. L. Goodhart
1953   The Queen's Peace by Sir Carleton Kemp Allen
1954   Executive Discretion and Judicial Control by Professor C. J. Hamson
1955   The Proof of Guilt by Professor Glanville Williams
1956   Trial by Jury by the Rt Hon. Lord Devlin
1957   Protection from Power under English Law by the Rt Hon. Lord MacDermott
1958   The Sanctity of Contracts in English Law by Professor Sir David Hughes Parry
1959   Judge and Jurist in the Reign of Victoria by C. H. S. Fifoot
1960   The Common Law in India by M. C. Setalvad
1961   British Justice: The Scottish Contribution by Professor Sir Thomas Smith
1962   Lawyer and Litigant in England by the Rt Hon. Sir Robert Megarry
1963   Crime and the Criminal Law by the Baroness Wootton of Abinger
1964   Law and Lawyers in the United States by Dean Erwin N. Griswold
1965   New Law for a New World? by the Rt Hon. Lord Tangley
1966   Other People's Law by the Rt Hon. Lord Kilbrandon

1967   The Contribution of English Law to South African
        Law: and the Rule of Law in South Africa by the
        Hon. O. D. Schreiner

1968   Justice in the Welfare State by Professor H. Street

1969   The British Tradition in Canadian Law by the
        Hon. Bora Laskin

1970   The English Judge by Henry Cecil

1971   Punishment, Prison and the Public by Professor Sir
        Rupert Cross

1972   Labour and the Law by Professor Sir Otto Kahn-Freund

1973   Maladministration and its Remedies by Sir Kenneth
        Wheare

1974   English Law – the New Dimension by the Rt Hon. Lord
        Scarman

1975   The Land and the Development; or, The Turmoil and the
        Torment by Sir Desmond Heap

1976   The National Insurance Commissioners by Sir Robert
        Micklethwait

1977   The European Communities and the Rule of Law by Lord
        Mackenzie Stuart

1978   Liberty, Law and Justice by Professor Sir Norman
        Anderson

1979   Social History and Law Reform by Professor Lord
        McGregor of Durris

1980   Constitutional Fundamentals by Professor Sir William
        Wade

1981   Intolerable Inquisition? Reflections on the Law of Tax by
        Hubert Monroe

1982   The Quest for Security: Employees, Tenants, Wives by
        Professor Tony Honoré

1983   Hamlyn Revisited: The British Legal System Today by
        Lord Hailsham of St Marylebone

1984   The Development of Consumer Law and Policy – Bold
        Spirits and Timorous Souls by Sir Gordon Borrie

1985   Law and Order by Professor Ralf Dahrendorf

1986   The Fabric of English Civil Justice by Sir Jack Jacob

1987   Pragmatism and Theory in English Law by Professor P. S. Atiyah

1988   Justification and Excuse in the Criminal Law by Professor J. C. Smith

1989   Protection of the Public – A New Challenge by the Rt Hon. Lord Justice Woolf

1990   The United Kingdom and Human Rights by Dr Claire Palley

1991   Introducing a European Legal Order by Gordon Slynn

1992   Speech and Respect by Professor Richard Abel

1993   The Administration of Justice by Lord Mackay of Clashfern

1994   Blackstone's Tower: The English Law School by Professor William Twining

1995   From the Test Tube to the Coffin: Choice and Regulation in Private Life by the Hon. Mrs Justice Hale

1996   Turning Points of the Common law by the Rt Hon. the Lord Cooke of Thorndon

1997   Commercial Law in the Next Millennium by Professor Roy Goode

1998   Freedom, Law and Justice by the Rt Hon. Lord Justice Sedley

1999   The State of Justice by Professor Michael Zander QC

2000   Does the United Kingdom still have a Constitution? by Professor Anthony King

2001   Human Rights, Serious Crime and Criminal Procedure by Professor Andrew Ashworth QC

2002   Legal Conundrums in our Brave New World by Baroness Kennedy of the Shaws

2003   Judicial Activism by the Hon. Justice Michael Kirby AC CMG

2004   Rights at Work: Global, European and British Perspectives by Sir Bob Hepple QC, FBA

2005	Can Human Rights Survive? by Professor Conor Gearty
2006	The Sovereignty of Law: The European Way by Sir Francis Jacobs KCMG, QC
2007	The Prisoners' Dilemma by Professor Nicola Lacey
2008	Judging Civil Justice by Dame Hazel Genn

1

'Foreign moods, fads, or fashions'

When Miss Hamlyn signed her will on 12 June 1939, less than three months before the Second World War began, the world was on the brink of radical change. But she was secure in her Britishness, confident in the superior virtue of the law developed in these islands. So, when bequeathing the residue of her will, she wished what she called 'the Common People of this country' to be instructed by lectures or otherwise in 'the Comparative Jurisprudence and the Ethnology of the chief European Countries including our own and the circumstances of the growth of such Jurisprudence', but she did so for a very specific purpose: 'to the intent that the Common People of our Country may realise the privileges which in law and custom they enjoy in comparison with other European Peoples and realising and appreciating such privileges may recognise the responsibilities and obligations attaching to them'. Thus Miss Hamlyn sought to promote responsible, law-abiding citizenship, and to do so by impressing on her British fellow-citizens the advantages their national law conferred on them as compared with their less fortunate European counterparts. So the jurisprudence of the chief European countries was firmly marked 'Not for import'. As Lord Hailsham once observed, 'Abroad is for hols.'

As the daughter of a solicitor practising in the West Country, who also sat as a Justice of the Peace for some years, Miss Hamlyn no doubt grew up with some knowledge of legal matters, and she is said to have studied the law herself, although little or nothing is known of her progress as a student. She was, however, described as 'very intellectual' and may therefore have warmed – unlike many practitioners – to the more philosophical aspects of the subject. Be that as it may, she clearly regarded our law in this country as something quite separate and distinct from the law of other countries. Her mental picture was of British (more probably, in truth, English) judges administering a body of indigenous, home-made law, some of it statutory, some of it made by the judges in case after case decided over the centuries, some of it customary, but all of it 'Made in Britain'.

This is a picture which very many people, including most judges and legal practitioners at the time, would have shared. And of course it was, and remains, in part an accurate picture. There are some areas of the law – one might instance taxation and social security – in which the task of the courts is essentially to interpret and apply the extremely detailed and complex statutory schemes which Parliament has laid down. The judge is unlikely to gain much help in resolving the problem before the court from consideration of analogous schemes in Germany or Australia or the United States. The greater the statutory content of the law in a particular field, the more likely, generally speaking, is this to be so. But in other areas of the law, and sometimes even in these, to an extent which Miss Hamlyn could not have dreamed of, the modern British judge sitting in a British court is not confined to administering a body of indigenous, home-made law. Frequently, and increasingly, the judge is administering a body of law which derives, directly or indirectly, from the European Union. Sometimes, and again (it

2

would seem) increasingly, the judge is interpreting and giving domestic effect to a rule of international law. Often, nowadays, the judge is ruling on claims pertaining to human rights, and is doing so by reference to rules which are international, not national, in origin. Sometimes, in seeking to resolve a problem in domestic law, the judge gains assistance or inspiration from considering the law of another country in which an apparently satisfactory solution to the same or a similar problem has been found. The task of the British judge is, as it has long been, to 'do right to all manner of people, after the laws and usages of this realm, without fear or favour, affection or ill-will', but 'the laws and usages of this realm' have a broader connotation today than they were thought to bear seventy years ago in 1939 when Miss Hamlyn laid down her pen. Judicial horizons have widened and are widening.

It is these widening horizons which I wish to discuss in these three chapters. In this first chapter I shall consider the use of comparative law in British courts. In the second chapter I shall address the modern role of the British courts in applying international law. In the third and final chapter I will touch on the role of the British courts in relation to the international law of human rights. I shall not address the first of the non-indigenous sources just mentioned, the law of the European Union. This is not because it is unimportant. Far from it. My reason for the omission is that this topic was addressed in the much-acclaimed Hamlyn Lectures (*The Sovereignty of Law*) given by Professor Sir Francis Jacobs in 2006 and any contribution by me would be a work of inexpert supererogation.

I turn, therefore, to the use of comparative law, by which I mean the law of other jurisdictions, in the British courts. In doing so, I should acknowledge at the outset the existence of a body of opinion which regards such law as at best irrelevant and at worst dangerous. Such was the view vividly expressed by Justice Scalia in the United States Supreme Court in a human rights context when he dismissed the majority's discussion of foreign authorities as 'meaningless dicta' and ruled that the court 'should not impose foreign moods, fads, or fashions on Americans'.[1] Others, more temperately, have drawn attention to the inevitable differences of legal culture, tradition, education and statutory background between one country and another, to the difficulty facing any practitioner or judge seeking to assimilate a foreign law in anything approaching an accurate or comprehensive way and to the even greater difficulties which arise where the foreign law is accessible to the judge or practitioner only through the medium of translation. These are real problems. Even where a decision is made in the English language and by a court (such as a state or federal court in the United States) exercising a recognisably similar jurisdiction, it is not always easy for the foreign lawyer to be sure whether the decision is representative of mainstream jurisprudence or the ill-considered work of some maverick judge; where a decision is based on the application of a foreign code, available only in translation, the pitfalls are even greater. Accusations of superficiality and cherry-picking may be made, perhaps with justification.

It is, however, the mission of the comparative legal scholar to acquire expert knowledge of the law of one or more

---

[1] *Lawrence et al.* v. *Texas* 539 US 558 (2003), 598, citing *Foster* v. *Florida* 537 US 990 (2002), note.

foreign countries as well as of his or her own country; to provide reliable translations and explanations of foreign materials; to place them in their historical and social context; to highlight differences and draw attention to similarities; to enable intelligent lawyers grappling with a problem in one country to see it through the eyes of a lawyer grappling with the same problem in another. Even expert scholarly guidance of this kind will not of course immunise practitioners or judges against the risk of error. But few human activities are free from the risk of error and judicial decision-making is no exception.

Those who see, and would wish to see, the law of England and Wales as 'an island, entire of it self' face two problems. The first is that, much as we (like Miss Hamlyn) may care to think of our law as a pure-bred, home-grown product of our national genius, the truth is otherwise. It is a mongrel, gaining in vigour and intelligence what it has lost in purity of pedigree. As a trading nation, we have not over the years been immune to foreign influences, but have responded to them when it appeared that a little discreet borrowing would improve our law.[2] There is perhaps no better example than the rule governing the measure of damages in contract, known to lawyers as 'the rule in *Hadley* v. *Baxendale*':[3] sometimes seen as a fine flowering of common law jurisprudence, the immediate sources of the rule were the French Code Civil, Pothier's *Treatise on the Law of Civil Obligations*, Kent's *Commentaries*[4]

---

[2] See the author's general discussion in ' "There is a World Elsewhere": The Changing Perspectives of English Law' in T. Bingham, *The Business of Judging* (Oxford University Press, 2000), 87–102.

[3] (1854) 9 Ex 341.

[4] (New York: D. Halsted, 1826–30), vol. II, 480.

and Sedgwick's *Treatise on Damages*,[5] none of them works of indigenous origin.[6]

The second problem faced by those who regard any resort to foreign sources as at best irrelevant and at worst dangerous is of a more general nature. In no other field of intellectual endeavour – be it science, medicine, philosophy, literature, architecture, art, music, engineering or sociology – would ideas or insights be rejected simply because they were of foreign origin. If, as most of us would probably like to think, the law is a humane science reflecting the product of intellectual endeavour century after century, it would be strange if in this field alone practitioners and academics were obliged to ignore developments elsewhere, or at least to regard them as of no practical consequence. Such an approach can only impoverish our law; it cannot enrich it.

Distinguished voices have been raised in support of this more open-minded approach. Thus Lord Goff of Chievely has written:

> I welcome unreservedly the study of comparative law. In my own work, I have done and continue to do my limited best to promote it, in every possible way … We encourage the study of other systems of law in our universities and in independent institutes; we promote exchanges of professors and students between universities in different European countries; we hold meetings between senior judges from our own and other European countries; we

---

[5] Theodore Sedgwick, *A Treatise on the Measure of Damages* (1st edn, New York, 1847; 2nd edn, 1852).

[6] A. W. B. Simpson, 'Innovation in Nineteenth Century Contract Law', *Law Quarterly Review* 91 (1975) 247–78, at 273–7.

even attempt to take advantage of principles from other
systems of law in our judgments, though I have learned
from experience that nobody should underestimate the
difficulties facing such an enterprise.[7]

In similar vein, Conseiller Guy Canivet, formerly President of
the French Cour de Cassation, now a member of the Conseil
Constitutionnel, said:

Citizens and judges of States which share more or less
similar cultures and enjoy an identical level of economic
development are less and less prone to accept that
situations which raise the same issues of fact will yield
different results because of the difference in the rules of
law to be applied. This is true in the field of bioethics,
in economic law and tort liability. In all these cases,
there is a trend, one might even say a strong demand,
that compatible solutions are reached, regardless of the
difference in the underlying applicable rules of law.[8]

If, however, it is true, as I think it is, that modern British judges
are on the whole more inclined than their forebears to consider the effect of foreign authority in appropriate cases, the
case should not be put too high. It is not easy, if indeed it is
possible, to identify cases in which resort to foreign authority (I am excluding cases relating to the law of the EU, international law and human rights law) can be confidently said

---

[7] 'Coming Together – the Future' in *The Coming Together of the Common
Law and the Civil Law,* The Clifford Chance Millennium Lectures, ed.
B. S. Markesinis (Oxford: Hart Publishing, 2000), 239–49, at 240–1.
[8] Lecture at the British Institute of International and Comparative Law,
November 2002.

to have had a decisive effect on the outcome in the sense that the judge would have decided differently but for the foreign authority. We should not, I think, regard foreign authority as a match-winner, a magical ace of trumps. But there are perhaps two situations in which foreign authority may exert a significant if not a decisive influence. One is where domestic authority points towards an answer that seems inappropriate or unjust. The other is where domestic authority appears to yield no clear answer. In such situations, as I shall seek to show, the courts have proved willing to take notice of, and give weight to, solutions developed elsewhere.

The first category, then, includes cases in which domestic authority points towards an answer that seems inappropriate or unjust. I will give three examples. The first is *Kleinwort Benson Limited* v. *Lincoln City Council and others*.[9] The facts, briefly summarised, were these. In the early 1980s Kleinwort Benson (which I shall call 'the bank') entered into rate swap agreements with the Lincoln City Council and three other local authorities. The agreements were duly performed and the bank paid the authorities a sum exceeding £800,000. Time passed until, in 1991, the House of Lords delivered an unexpected judgment holding rate swap agreements to be unlawful as outside the powers of the local authorities.[10] The bank sued the local authorities to recover the sums overpaid, and succeeded in recovering sums paid within the six-year limitation period.

---

[9] [1999] 2 AC 349.
[10] *Hazell* v. *Hammersmith and Fulham London Borough Council* [1992] 2 AC 1.

But recovery of the sums paid longer ago was problematical because of a well-established rule of English law which provided that, although money paid under a mistake of fact could be recovered, money paid under a mistake of law could not. That rule was very pertinent here, since the bank had paid out under the agreements in the belief that it was legally obliged to do so. Until the House of Lords judgment in 1991, that was a very reasonable belief.

Now I venture to think that the Common People of this country, Miss Hamlyn's chosen audience, would be puzzled by this rule. The local authorities had received money to which they were not entitled. The limitation period could be extended if the bank had paid under a mistake which it could not with reasonable diligence have discovered earlier.[11] If the bank had sent its payment to the wrong authority under a mistake of fact, it could have recovered it. Why should the local authorities hang on to money to which they were not entitled simply because the bank had, entirely reasonably, shared what was at the time a settled understanding of the law?

At first instance the judge decided this issue against the bank, as he was bound to do, and when its appeal reached the House of Lords a minority of two out of five law lords agreed with him. But a majority, led by Lord Goff in an opinion of outstanding quality, held that the existing rule should be abrogated. What matters for present purposes is that Lord Goff, in reaching his conclusion, supplemented his discussion of English authority by referring to the American Law Institute's *Restatement of the Law, Restitution* (1937), and to

---

[11] Section 32(1)(c) of the Limitation Act 1980.

9

authority deriving from Canada, Australia, South Africa, the United States, Germany, Italy and France.[12] This enabled Lord Goff to say:

> For present purposes, however, the importance of this comparative material is to reveal that, in civil law systems, a blanket exclusion of recovery of money paid under a mistake of law is not regarded as necessary. In particular, the experience of these systems assists to dispel the fears expressed in the early English cases that a right of recovery on the ground of mistake of law may lead to a flood of litigation, while at the same time it shows that in some cases a right of recovery, which has in the past been denied by the mistake of law rule, may likewise be denied in civil law countries on the basis of a narrower ground of principle or policy.[13]

In deciding what rule should be laid down here, Lord Goff referred to legislation in New Zealand and Western Australia[14] and to reports of the Law Commissions not only of England and Wales[15] but also of British Columbia, New Zealand, South Australia, New South Wales and Scotland.[16] Lord Hoffmann described this as one of 'the most distinguished' of Lord Goff's 'luminous contributions to this branch of the law',[17] and it gained immeasurable strength from the world-wide perspective which he adopted.

---

[12] [1992] 2 AC 349, at 373–5.
[13] *Ibid.* at 375 C.
[14] *Ibid.* at 374, 384.
[15] *Ibid.* at 372, 376–7.
[16] *Ibid.* at 384.
[17] *Ibid.* at 398.

My second example under this head is of an entirely different character. It concerns the advocate's immunity from claims for negligence arising out of the conduct of proceedings in court. This immunity had been affirmed by the House of Lords in 1967 in *Rondel* v. *Worsley*,[18] the well-known case in which a defendant, who admitted biting off his victim's earlobe and injuring his hand, sought to blame his barrister for his conviction and consequent imprisonment. In that and a later case[19] the immunity was firmly grounded on considerations of public policy. But it had come to be questioned why advocates, alone among professionals, should be granted a degree of protection denied to others (such as doctors and social workers) called upon to make difficult and contentious decisions. It looked a little as if lawyers – as usual, some would say – were looking after themselves. In a group of three appeals, known by the name of the first, *Arthur J. S. Hall & Co.* v. *Simons*,[20] the immunity was challenged. The problem was not that domestic authority offered no answer, but that the answer (as far as it applied to the conduct of court proceedings) no longer seemed obviously appropriate, or just, or warranted by the public policy considerations said to underpin it, which were the undesirability of relitigating matters already the subject of court decision, the protection against civil liability of those participating in court proceedings and the special duty owed by an advocate to the court, sometimes superseding the duty owed to his client. An enlarged panel of seven Law Lords was

[18] [1969] 1 AC 191.
[19] *Saif Ali* v. *Sydney Mitchell & Co.* [1980] AC 198.
[20] [2002] 1 AC 615.

convened to decide this challenge to what, by legal standards, was quite recent authority.

In his leading opinion Lord Steyn noted that whereas, in 1967 in *Rondel* v. *Worsley*, the House had had no comparative material placed before it, the House had in the present case had 'the benefit of a substantial comparative review'.[21] He noted that *Rondel* v. *Worsley* had been followed at the highest level in Australia and New Zealand, but also noted that in the countries of the European Union advocates enjoyed no immunity. There were, of course, important differences of trial procedure between civil and common law jurisdictions, but the absence of immunity in those countries had apparently caused no practical difficulties. In the United States prosecutors had an immunity, extended in some states to public defenders, but otherwise lawyers were not protected against claims for negligence by their clients. Most significantly, in Lord Steyn's opinion, advocates in Canada had no immunity from actions for negligence before *Rondel* v. *Worsley*. The question was closely examined following that decision,[22] but no evidence was found that the work of Canadian courts was hampered in any way by counsel's fear of civil liability and *Rondel* v. *Worsley* was not followed. The Canadian experience, Lord Steyn concluded, tended to show that those who thought abrogation of the rule would undermine the public interest were unnecessarily pessimistic. If the public policy reasons relied on to support the rule did not accord with experience in a country as like our own as Canada, it was indeed difficult to

[21] *Ibid.* at 680 G.
[22] *Demarco* v. *Ungaro* (1979) 95 DLR (3d) 385, followed in later cases.

see why they should apply here, and that was what a majority of the House decided.

My third example under this head is again a case of quite a different character. It is *Fairchild* v. *Glenhaven Funeral Services Ltd*,[23] the first of three appeals heard together in the House of Lords. The facts of the cases were simple and stark. A number of workmen had over a period of years worked in the asbestos industry for a series of employers, all of whom had exposed the men to unlawful levels of asbestos dust. All the men had contracted a form of cancer (a mesothelioma) caused by inhalation of asbestos dust or fibre. When the appeals were heard, some had already died; others were dying; the condition was incurable. But the evidence showed that this form of cancer could, as probably as not, be caused by inhalation of a single fibre of asbestos. It was not a condition to which each exposure contributed in a cumulative way. The problem which the claimants faced was that they could not show which employer they had been working for at the time when they inhaled the fatal fibre, and thus could not identify the particular defendant who had caused their condition.

This was not a situation in which the ordinary rules of domestic law offered no answer. They offered a clear answer: that the claims had to fail because the claimants could not establish a chain of causation linking the admittedly unlawful conduct of any particular defendant with the injury of which the particular claimant complained. That was the answer which the Court of Appeal gave,[24] sending the men

---

23 [2002] UKHL 22, [2003] 1 AC 32.
24 [2002] 1 WLR 1052, [2002] ICR 412.

away empty-handed. This decision represented a logical application of legal principle, but one might question whether Miss Hamlyn's Common People would have thought it very just, and it did not seem so to the Appellate Committee of the House of Lords. In agreeing that the appeals should be allowed, Lord Nicholls considered that 'Any other outcome would be deeply offensive to instinctive notions of what justice requires and fairness demands.'[25]

The House of Lords in their opinions reviewed English, Australian, Canadian and Scottish authority, but some Law Lords also touched on European and other materials which they had invited counsel to explore. Thus reference was made to leading textbooks on the European law of torts, and to materials from Germany, Greece, Austria, The Netherlands, France, Spain, Norway, Italy, Switzerland, South Africa, California and the American Law Institute, *Restatement of the Law of Torts* 2d (2nd edn, 1965). I ventured to summarise what seemed, and still seems, to me to be the correct approach in situations of this kind:

> Development of the law in this country cannot of course
> depend on a head-count of decisions and codes adopted
> in other countries around the world, often against a
> background of different rules and traditions. The law must
> be developed coherently, in accordance with principle, so
> as to serve, even-handedly, the ends of justice. If, however,
> a decision is given in this country which offends one's
> basic sense of justice, and if consideration of international
> sources suggests that a different and more acceptable

---

[25] [2002] UKHL 22, [2003] 1 AC 32, at 68.

decision would be given in most other jurisdictions, whatever their legal tradition, this must prompt anxious review of the decision in question. In a shrinking world (in which the employees of asbestos companies may work for those companies in any one or more of several countries) there must be some virtue in uniformity of outcome whatever the diversity of approach in reaching that outcome.[26]

This foray into comparative European law has not escaped criticism. A distinguished Cambridge scholar was dismissive:

The *tour d'horizon* attempted by the House of Lords was admittedly superficial. Omitted is the salient fact that in almost none of the jurisdictions glanced at would the claimants in *Fairchild* have succeeded: in most places an employee cannot simply sue his employer in tort, since workmen's compensation or social security takes its place.[27]

This conclusion has itself been the subject of authoritative criticism, and may not be correct.[28] But if the *tour d'horizon* was superficial, that is a defect in the execution, not the method. If the foreign principles were correctly summarised, it matters little that the foreign claimants would have been compensated under an overriding statutory scheme. And the inescapable question remains whether men who had lost their health and

---

[26] *Ibid.* at 66.

[27] Tony Weir, 'Making it More Likely v. Making it Happen', *Cambridge Law Journal* [2002] 519–22.

[28] B. S. Markesinis, 'Goethe, Bingham, and the Gift of an Open Mind' in *Tom Bingham and the Transformation of the Law* (Oxford University Press, 2009), 729–49, at 740–2.

their lives through the unlawful conduct of another should have been sent away with no more than the state benefit to which they were entitled.

So much, then, for my first category, cases in which domestic authority points towards an answer that seems inappropriate. I turn to the second, cases in which domestic authority appears to yield no clear answer. Again, I suggest, foreign authority can help to guide the British judge towards a solution. I cite examples.

My first example, *Henderson* v. *Merrett Syndicates Ltd*,[29] concerned a dispute between Lloyd's Names and their agents. Happily, the details of the dispute do not matter for present purposes. One of the questions which arose, a technical but also an important one, was whether a claimant could sue both in tort, alleging breach of a tortious duty of care, and also, concurrently, in contract, asserting a similar duty. English law appeared to give an uncertain and rather unprincipled answer. So Lord Goff turned to foreign authority, noting that, although French law required a claimant to pursue his remedy in contract alone, this rule was not followed in all civil law jurisdictions, notably Germany, and that no perceptible harm had come to the German system from admitting concurrent claims.[30] So Lord Goff, after reviewing domestic authority, considered authority emanating from Ireland, Canada, New Zealand, Australia and the United States, in most of which reliance on concurrent causes of action was coming to be accepted, although a claimant could not escape the effect

---

[29] [1995] 2 AC 145.
[30] *Ibid*. at 184.

16

of a contractual exclusion on limitation of liability by suing in tort.[31] At the end of his survey Lord Goff concluded:

> My own belief is that, in the present context, the common law is not antipathetic to concurrent liability, and that there is no sound basis for a rule which automatically restricts the claimant to either a tortious or a contractual remedy. The result may be untidy; but, given that the tortious duty is imposed by the general law, and that the contractual duty is attributable to the will of the parties, I do not find it objectionable that the claimant may be entitled to take advantage of the remedy which is most advantageous to him, subject only to ascertaining whether the tortious duty is so inconsistent with the applicable contract that, in accordance with ordinary principle, the parties must be taken to have agreed that the tortious remedy is to be limited or excluded.[32]

The second example, *White* v. *Jones*,[33] is well known. Following a family row, a father made a will excluding his two daughters from any share in his estate. When the row subsided, he gave oral and written instructions to a legal executive (Mr Jones), employed by a solicitor, to draw up a new will, under which each of the daughters was to receive £9,000. But Mr Jones was dilatory in acting on these instructions, and before he did so the father died with the earlier will unrevoked. Thus each of the daughters lost the £9,000 which, as they knew, they were each to inherit under the new will. There was an earlier, first

---

[31] *Ibid.* at 191–2.
[32] *Ibid.* at 193–4.
[33] [1995] 2 AC 207.

instance, decision on very similar facts, holding that the disappointed beneficiary could recover damages in negligence,[34] but domestic authority did not speak with one voice and opinion elsewhere was divided. There were, moreover, conceptual problems facing the claimant, among them that a solicitor acting on behalf of a client ordinarily owes a duty only to that client; that a solicitor's duty is ordinarily said to lie in contract, not tort; and that, if the claims succeeded, the beneficiaries would recover more than had ever been in the father's estate, there being no ground for denying the entitlement of the beneficiaries under the earlier, entirely valid will. These difficulties led to a division of opinion in the House of Lords. On the other hand, there was what Lord Goff described as 'the extraordinary fact'[35] that, if a duty were not held to be owed by Mr Jones to the daughters, 'the only persons who might have a valid claim (i.e., the testator and his estate) have suffered no loss, and the only person who has suffered a loss (i.e. the disappointed beneficiary) has no claim'.

In approaching this problem Lord Goff considered the law laid down in New Zealand, Canada, the United States, Germany, France, The Netherlands, Victoria, Western Australia, Tasmania and the High Court of Australia.[36] But he derived particular help from the German experience. In doing so, he sounded a note of warning:

> Strongly though I support the study of comparative law,
> I hesitate to embark in an opinion such as this upon

---

[34] *Ross* v. *Caunters* [1980] Ch. 297.
[35] [1995] 2 AC 207, at 259 G.
[36] *Ibid.* at 254–64.

18

a comparison, however brief, with a civil law system; because experience has taught me how very difficult, and indeed potentially misleading, such an exercise can be. Exceptionally however, in the present case, thanks to material published in our language by distinguished comparatists, German as well as English, we have direct access to publications which should sufficiently dispel our ignorance of German law and so by comparison illuminate our understanding of our own.[37]

Thus armed – in particular by the work of Professor Werner Lorenz[38] and Professor Basil Markesinis[39] – Lord Goff drew inspiration from German doctrines which, in the face of a rule that a claim will not lie in delict (or tort) to recover damages for pure economic loss in negligence, have provided a remedy of a contractual nature in such situations. The German names for these doctrines (*Schutzwirkung für Dritte*, 'contract with protective effect for third parties', and *Drittschadensliquidation*, 'available in cases of transferred loss') convey the flavour of their effect. Applying these principles by analogy to the cases of the disappointed daughters, Lord Goff reached a conclusion which he judged to produce practical justice for all parties concerned,[40] a conclusion with which a majority of his colleagues agreed. One may infer that Miss Hamlyn also

---

[37] *Ibid.* at 263 B.
[38] 'Contracts and Third-Party Rights in German and English Law' in *The Gradual Convergence*, ed. B. Markesinis (Oxford University Press, 1994), at 65–97; *Essays in Memory of Professor F. H. Lawson* (1986), 86, 89–90.
[39] *The Gradual Convergence*, above; *The German Law of Torts* (3rd edn, Oxford University Press, 1994).
[40] [1995] 2 AC 207, at 268 F.

would have agreed, unless her loyalty as a solicitor's daughter led her to demur.

The main issue raised in my third example, *Hunter v. Canary Wharf Ltd*[41] was whether occupiers of premises in the Docklands redevelopment area of east London could claim in private nuisance because the Canary Wharf Tower, a massive building, interfered with the television reception at their homes. This was, for obvious reasons, a rather novel problem, although a judge in 1964, while rejecting the claim before him, had accepted the possibility that ability to receive television signals free from interference might one day be recognised as 'so important a part of an ordinary householder's enjoyment of his property that such interference should be regarded as a legal nuisance'.[42] The problem in the case was that all the developers had done was erect a building, on their own land, in accordance with planning permission, as they had every right to do. A subsidiary problem was whether a claimant must have an interest in land to sue in private nuisance.

Again, it was Lord Goff who led the comparative survey, summarising the leading English cases, but also considering authority from Canada, New Zealand and, particularly, Germany,[43] to conclude, on the first point, that no action lay in private nuisance for interference with television caused by the mere presence of a building. But the subsidiary issue also called for consideration of authority emanating from New

---

[41] [1997] AC 655.
[42] *Bridlington Relay Ltd v. Yorkshire Electricity Board* [1965] Ch 436, 447, per Buckley J.
[43] [1997] AC 655, at 685–7.

Zealand, Victoria, Alberta, New Brunswick[44] and (in the opinion of Lord Cooke, dissenting on this point)[45] Alberta, New Brunswick, the United States, Australia and Scotland. In the result, the majority overruled in part an earlier decision of the Court of Appeal,[46] preferring to adhere to what the law had previously been thought to be and unpersuaded that the law should be extended.

McFarlane v. Tayside Health Board,[47] my fourth example, raised a problem of an unusually sensitive and difficult nature. A married couple with four children wished to have no more children, and, to preclude that possibility, the husband underwent a vasectomy operation, following which they were advised that contraceptive measures were no longer necessary. The operation had been negligently performed, or the advice negligently given, and the wife conceived and gave birth to a healthy child. It was held that the wife could recover damages against the Health Board, for the inconvenience of pregnancy and childbirth, but the more difficult and divisive question was whether the parents could recover the full cost of rearing the child until the age of maturity. The claim was brought in Scotland, and the judge at first instance rejected this latter claim, ruling that a pregnancy, even if undesired, was not a personal injury for which damages could be recovered, and that in any event the rewards of parenthood outweighed any financial loss. The Inner House of the Court of Session, on appeal, took a different view: if negligence were

---

44 *Ibid.* at 689–94.
45 *Ibid.* at 714–23.
46 *Khorasandjian v. Bush* [1993] QB 727.
47 [2000] 2 AC 59.

21

established, the parents were entitled to recover as damages the loss foreseeably caused to them as a result. Both approaches have attractions. The decision of the Inner House, allowing full recovery, was an orthodox application of familiar and conventional principles of the law of tort.[48] But considerations of legal policy weighed against treating the birth of a healthy child as a financial burden and nothing more.[49] When the Health Board's appeal reached the House of Lords, it was necessary for a choice to be made.

The same problem had arisen elsewhere. So it was that Lord Slynn referred to cases in the United States, South Africa, New Zealand, New South Wales, France, Germany and The Netherlands,[50] Lord Steyn to authority in the United States, Canada, New Zealand, Australia, Germany and France,[51] Lord Hope to authority in Scotland, Canada, the United States, South Africa and Australia, Lord Clyde to authority in Canada, Scotland, New Zealand and the United States,[52] and Lord Millett to authority in the United States, Canada, Australia and New Zealand.[53] This survey made clear that different courts had expressed a wide range of opinions, unsurprisingly in a matter of this kind where ethical and moral as well as purely legal considerations could influence the view taken. Thus there was no uniformity of outcome across the world, and indeed

---

[48] See *Rees* v. *Darlington Memorial Hospital NHS Trust* [2003] UKHL 52, [2004] 1 AC 309, para. 4, per Lord Bingham.

[49] *Ibid.*, para. 6.

[50] [2000] 2 AC 59, at 71–3.

[51] *Ibid.* at 80–3.

[52] *Ibid.* at 99–106.

[53] *Ibid.* at 108–13.

the High Court of Australia, by a bare majority, later took a view different from the House of Lords by upholding a claim for full recovery.[54] But, as already suggested, the purpose of recourse to comparative jurisprudence is not to conduct an international opinion poll. Its value and use may differ from case to case. Here, however, it is hard to suppose that the opinions of their Lordships were not strengthened and refined by the opportunity which they had enjoyed of studying the reasoning of other courts confronting the same problem as they had to resolve, whether in the event they agreed with that reasoning or not.

My fifth and final example is a first-instance decision, little noted save by comparatists:[55] *Greatorex* v. *Greatorex*.[56] It was given by Cazalet J, a judge of the Family Division, and sounds from its title like a family case. But it was not. The claimant was a professional fire officer, called to the scene of a serious motor accident in which the primary victim was his son. The son had been driving the crashed car and it was his negligent driving – overtaking on the blind brow of a hill – which had led to the collision with an oncoming car. This exposure to his son's injuries caused the father to suffer long-term, severe, post-traumatic stress disorder. He sued his son to recover damages for this psychiatric injury, but the son was

---

54 *Cattanach* v. *Melchior* [2003] HCA 38.
55 See, for example, B. S. Markesinis, 'Foreign Law Inspiring National Law. Lessons from *Greatorex v Greatorex*' in *Comparative Law in the Courtroom and Classroom* (Oxford: Hart Publishing, 2003), 157–82; B. S. Markesinis with Jörg Fedtke, *Engaging with Foreign Law* (Oxford: Hart Publishing, 2009), ch. 9.
56 [2000] 1 WLR 1970.

uninsured, so the cudgels were taken up on his behalf by the Motor Insurers' Bureau. The issue which arose, ordered to be tried as a preliminary issue, was in essence whether a victim of self-inflicted injuries (i.e. injuries caused to the victim by his own negligence) owed a duty of care to a third party not to cause him psychiatric injury.

There was no English authority establishing such liability,[57] and while dicta suggested that a claim would probably not succeed they also recognised the logical problems and anomalies inherent in that view.[58] A line of Australian authority, discussed in some detail by Cazalet J, ruled out such liability, as did a decision of the Supreme Court of British Columbia,[59] but the judge recognised that liability for psychiatric injury – or nervous shock as it was once called – was a field in which the courts had laid down restrictive rules to limit the class of secondary claimants who could be entitled to recover. Thus a claimant must have close ties of love and affection with the primary victim, must have been present at the accident or its immediate aftermath and must have witnessed, not heard about, the accident or its aftermath.[60] These were limitations imposed by legal policy. But Mr Greatorex satisfied them.[61] Was he, on grounds of English legal policy, to be excluded from the right to recover because his psychiatric

---

[57] *Alcock* v. *Chief Constable of South Yorkshire* [1992] 1 AC 310, 401 C, per Lord Ackner.

[58] See Lord Oliver, *ibid.* at 418 B–H.

[59] [2001] 1 WLR at 1980–2.

[60] *Ibid.*; *Frost* v. *Chief Constable of South Yorkshire Police* [1999] 2 AC 455, 502 per Lord Hoffmann.

[61] See [2000] 1 WLR 1970, at 1977 B.

injury was caused by exposure to the results of the negligent driving of his own son?

That was the question the judge addressed.[62] In doing so, he began by citing a 1971 decision of the German Bundes-gerichtshof (Sixth Civil Division) in which the facts were very similar.[63] The judgment contained a very clear statement:

> A person is under no legal duty, whatever the moral position may be, to look after his own life and limb simply in order to save his dependants from the likely psychical effects on them if he is killed or maimed: to impose such a legal duty, except in very peculiar cases, for instance, wherever a person commits suicide in a deliberately shocking manner, would be to restrict a person's self-determination in a manner inconsistent with our legal system.

The judge found force in this argument, and also considered, since close family ties are in any event a condition of recovery, that any other rule would encourage litigation within the family of a particularly undesirable kind.[64] Thus, guided by the German decision, the judge concluded that the son had in the circumstances owed no duty of care to the father.[65]

I conclude with a legal morality tale. In a series of three cases, all involving claims by shipowners against defaulting charterers, the question arose whether the English court could grant an injunction to restrain the charterer, who was

---

[62] *Ibid.* at 1983–7.

[63] *Hu. w. Ha*, translated by Mr Tony Weir and published in Markesinis, *The German Law of Torts*, 3rd edn, 109.

[64] [2000] 1 WLR 1970, at 1985 E.

[65] *Ibid.* at 1987 F–H.

not in the jurisdiction of the court but had assets within it, from removing those assets abroad before any claim had been established against him. In the first case of the three,[66] an ex parte application, the court understood that no such injunction had ever been granted. No authority was cited, but Lord Denning MR (whose homely language may blind later generations to his great erudition, something well known to those regularly appearing before him) rather grandly declared: 'We know, of course, that the practice on the continent of Europe is different. It seems to me that the time has come when we should revise our practice.'[67] An injunction was granted. In the second case,[68] no reference was made to foreign practice, but again an injunction was granted on an ex parte application, despite some doubt about the effect of earlier English authority, because the commercial situation appeared to call for injunctive relief. In the third case,[69] the court's power to grant an interlocutory injunction in such circumstances was seriously challenged. Lord Denning responded by referring to the old procedure of foreign attachment in the City of London, which permitted seizure of the goods within the jurisdiction of a defendant out of the jurisdiction as soon as a plaint had been issued.[70] This practice, he recorded, had been exported to the

---

[66] *Nippon Yusen Kaisha v. Karageorgis* [1975] 1 WLR 1093.

[67] *Ibid.* at 1094–5.

[68] *Mareva Compania Naviera SA v. International Bulkcarriers Ltd* [1975] 2 Lloyd's Rep 509.

[69] *Rasu Maritima SA v. Perusahaan Pertambangan Minyak Dan Gas Bumi Negara (Government of the Republic of Indonesia Intervening)* [1978] QB 644.

[70] *Ibid.* at 656–7.

United States and given legislative effect in a number of states. Citing a nineteenth-century author, Lord Denning said:

> In the extract which I have read from Pulling he says that the same process was available in most maritime towns on the continent of Europe. There it has survived most vigorously and is in force everywhere today. It is called in France 'saisie conservatoire'. It is applied universally on the continent. It enables the seizure of assets so as to preserve them for the benefit of the creditor. Very often the debtor lodges security and gets the assets released. Now that we have joined the common market, it would be appropriate that we should follow suit.[71]

That is not, however, the end of the story. For although the *saisie conservatoire*, as operated in France, provided an effective means of freezing assets within the territorial jurisdiction of France, French law offered no means by which a court could prevent the untimely removal of or interference with assets outside France. The problem became acute in a case concerning two art dealers domiciled in Paris who possessed immovable assets in Spain. How to resolve? The answer given by the Court of Appeal of Versailles, approved in principle by the Cour de Cassation following submissions by the Advocate-General, was: borrow from the English.[72] As the Cour de Cassation economically put it, rejecting an

---

[71] *Ibid.* at 658.

[72] Cass. civ. 1ère 19 Nov. 2002, *Banque Worms* (2002) JCP 10 201 concl. Sainte-Rose, note Chaillé de Néré [2003] D 797 note Khainallah; and see generally H. Muir Watt, 'Of Transcultural Borrowing, Hybrids, and the Complexity of Legal Knowledge' in *Comparative Law Before the Courts*, ed. G. Canivet, M. Andenas and D. Fairgrieve (BIICL, 2004) 35–48.

argument based on the territorial limits of the court, 'an injunction addressed to the defendant personally to act or refrain from acting, wherever the assets are situated, does not fall foul of such jurisdictional limits, as long as it is awarded by the court with legitimate jurisdiction over the merits'. Could there be a better example of constructive, international cross-fertilisation? One likes to think that Miss Hamlyn's heart would rejoice.

2

'Wider still and wider'

The theme of this volume, a little inconsistently perhaps with Miss Hamlyn's patriotic vision, is that British judges, sitting in British courts today, to an extent which she could scarcely have imagined, take note of and apply laws which are not indigenous to the United Kingdom, whose provenance is elsewhere. In the first chapter I discussed some cases – of course, a small minority of all cases decided – in which courts called on to resolve vexatious problems here were assisted towards a solution by consideration of the reasoning of foreign courts faced with the same problems. In this chapter I seek to address, necessarily briefly, the impact of international law on the work of the British courts.

It seems unlikely that international law loomed large in the consciousness of the Common People whom Miss Hamlyn wished her lectures to address, or for that matter in her own. Indeed, at the time when she made her will, and later, there were those, distinguished lawyers among them, who argued that international law was no law at all. And of course it is true that international law lacks some of the features which we most closely associate with domestic legal process: a representative assembly to lay down the law, a compulsory process of adjudication and an effective means of enforcement. But despite, and in large part because of, the breathtaking technological advances which have taken place in the seventy years since Miss Hamlyn laid down her pen in June 1939, the world has shrunk. There were always, of course, problems such as piracy which could only be effectively addressed by different nations, acting in concert, according to rules internationally agreed. But the number of such problems has increased exponentially over the years. A recent book lists the main practice areas in which issues of international law may arise.[1] They include aviation, commercial and intellectual property law, criminal law, employment and industrial relations law, environmental law, family and child law, human rights law, immigration and asylum law, immunities and privileges, international organisations, jurisdiction, law of the sea, treaties, warfare and weapons law. There are international courts and tribunals which have limited jurisdiction in these areas, notably the International Court of Justice but also bodies such as the World Trade Organization, the International Centre for the Settlement of Investment Disputes, various human rights adjudicative bodies and many more. But the application of international law is not the exclusive preserve of these bodies. Increasingly, national courts are called on to play a part. And this, I suggest, is to be welcomed: we all have an interest in due observance of the rules which govern life on the international, as on the national, plane.

By international law I mean, with no claim to originality, international conventions establishing rules expressly recognised by the parties to them, international custom as evidence of a general practice accepted as law, the general principles of law recognised by civilised nations, authoritative

---

[1] Shaheed Fatima, *Using International Law in Domestic Courts* (Oxford: Hart Publishing, 2005), 3–26.

judicial decisions and the writing of the most highly qualified international lawyers.[2] Lord Mansfield, drawing on earlier authority[3] and echoed by later judges,[4] famously declared that the law of nations – the old name for international law – was in its full extent part of the law of England,[5] and to the extent that that is so it can be argued that British judges, applying international law, are applying domestic law, whatever its origin. But this statement is true only of customary international law – general practice accepted as law among the nations – and for practical domestic purposes it is the laws deriving from treaties, or conventions, which are of the greatest significance.

In some instances, domestic effect is given by statute to a multilateral convention ratified by the United Kingdom, and then the statute has the same effect as any other. But it is worth noting the hostility which this process not infrequently attracts. In retrospect, it would be hard to imagine a field in which the need for a code of rules, internationally agreed among trading and maritime nations, was more obvious than the international carriage of goods by sea. It can make no sense that the rights and duties of shipowners and cargo-owners should depend on the law prevailing in a particular port at which the vessel has loaded or discharged her cargo. Yet the proposal to give domestic effect to the Hague Rules, negotiated at an international conference and in due course embodied in

---

[2] This is the broad effect of Article 38(1) of the Statute of the International Court of Justice, generally accepted as describing the sources of international law.

[3] *Barbuit's Case in Chancery* (1737) Forr. 280.

[4] Sir George Cornewall Lewis, *Lewis on Foreign Jurisdiction* (1859), 66–7.

[5] *Triquet* v. *Bath* (1764) 3 Burr 1478.

the Carriage of Goods by Sea Act 1924, was described by the leading authorities of the day as 'a terrifying prospect' and to the majority of legal opinion until the mid-1950s multilateral treaties were 'anathema'.[6]

The Hague Rules proved in practice to be very efficacious, and today, eighty-five years later, the 'almost hysterical' opposition to the 1924 Act seems, as Lord Roskill was later to say, 'astonishing',[7] and a later revision of the Rules, the Visby Protocol negotiated in 1968, was given statutory effect in 1971.[8] But, and this is the important point for present purposes, when construing a UK statute giving effect to an international convention, a British court does not interpret the statute as if it were a purely domestic instrument. Thus, as Lord Steyn made clear in a recent case,

> It has often been explained that the Hague Rules and Hague-Visby Rules represented a pragmatic compromise between the interests of owners, shippers and consignees. The Hague Rules were designed to achieve a part harmonisation of the diverse laws of trading nations.[9]

Lord Steyn was unwilling to displace an interpretation of one clause by Devlin J in 1954[10] which had not been based on linguistic matters but on the 'broad object of the Rules', not on

---

[6] This topic is illuminatingly discussed, with particular reference to the Vienna Sales Convention, by Johan Steyn, 'A Kind of Esperanto?' in *Democracy through Law* (Farnham: Ashgate, 2004), 245–51.

[7] *Law Quarterly Review* 108 (1992) 501.

[8] Carriage of Goods by Sea Act 1971.

[9] *Jindal Iron and Steel Co. Ltd* v. *Islamic Solidarity Shipping Co. Jordan Inc.* [2004] UKHL 49, [2005] 1 WLR 1363, para. 19.

[10] In *Pyrene Co. Ltd* v. *Scindia Navigation Co. Ltd* [1954] 2 QB 402.

'any technical rules of English law' but on 'a perspective relevant to the interests of maritime nations generally.'[11]

A somewhat similar process can be seen at work in the very different field of child abduction. Again there is an international convention (the Hague Convention on the Civil Aspects of International Child Abduction) and a UK statute (the Child Abduction and Custody Act 1985). But again, as with the Hague Rules, there is no supranational court charged with interpreting the Convention in a manner binding on contracting states. Yet as Lord Browne-Wilkinson pointed out in 1997,

> An international convention, expressed in different languages and intended to apply to a wide range of differing legal systems, cannot be construed differently in different jurisdictions. The Convention must have the same meaning and effect under the laws of all contracting states.[12]

This means, as the Court of Appeal has pointed out, that 'normally terms which have different meanings under the laws of contracting states will be given an autonomous Hague Convention interpretation.'[13] The task of the British and other national courts, taking account of the objects of the Convention, explanatory materials, decisions of courts around the world and relevant learned literature, is to identify and give effect to that autonomous meaning.

[11] *Jindal*, para. 19.
[12] *In re H (Minors) (Abduction: Acquiescence)* [1998] AC 72, 87.
[13] *In re P (A Child) (Abduction: Custody Rights)* [2004] EWCA Civ 971, [2005] Fam 293, para. 40.

The task of the court is facilitated by the clarity of Article 1 of the Convention:

> The objects of the present convention are – (a) to secure the prompt return of children wrongfully removed to or retained in any contracting state; and (b) to ensure that rights of custody and of access under the law of one contracting state are effectively respected in other contracting states.

The Convention was motivated by the

> belief that it is in the best interests of children for disputes about their future to be decided in their home countries, and that one parent should not be able to take a child from one country to another, either in the hope of obtaining a tactical advantage in the dispute or to avoid the effects of an order made in the home country. Instead of deciding the dispute itself, therefore, the country to which the child was taken agreed that with very few exceptions it would either send the child back or enforce the order made in the home country.[14]

In this context the welfare of the child, paramount in most proceedings affecting children, is overridden.

By Article 3, 'The removal or retention of a child' is to be considered wrongful where 'it is in breach of rights attributed to a person ... under the law of the state in which the child was habitually resident immediately before the removal or retention'. Where a child has been wrongfully removed and

---

[14] *In re J (A Child) (Custody Rights: Jurisdiction)* [2005] UKHL 40, [2006] 1 AC 80, para. 20.

34

application under the Convention is made within one year, the return of the child shall be ordered 'forthwith', but if more than a year has elapsed, the return of the child shall also be ordered, 'unless it is demonstrated that the child is now settled in its new environment' (Article 12). And, by Article 13, notwithstanding these provisions, a state is not bound to order the return of a child if the person opposing return establishes that the person having the care of the child consented to or acquiesced in the removal or that there is a grave risk that his or her return 'would expose the child to physical or psychological harm or otherwise place the child in an intolerable situation'. Return may also be refused if it is found that the child objects to being returned and has attained an age and degree of maturity at which it is appropriate to take account of his or her views.

These provisions, clear and well-drafted though they are, have given rise to a stream of questions which the British courts, searching for the autonomous meaning of the Convention, have answered. Brief examples may be given. Are the expressions 'rights of custody' and 'rights attributed to a person' to be judged according to English law or the law of the foreign state, or neither? The answer given was that the court must establish the right of the parent under the law of the foreign state and then consider whether those rights are rights of custody under the autonomous Hague Convention meaning.[15] In reaching this conclusion, the Court of Appeal considered decisions in Ireland, the United States, South Africa and Canada. Considering a related question, the House of Lords reviewed authorities from Scotland, the United States, New Zealand,

---

[15]   *Re P*, n. 13 above, para. 60.

Israel, Australia, Romania, South Africa and Canada.[16] When could a parent be held to have acquiesced in the removal or retention of a child? The House of Lords answered this question, taking account of decisions in the French Cour de Cassation, the District Court of Massachusetts and the US Court of Appeals of the Sixth Circuit.[17] If application for the return of a child is made after the expiration of one year and the child is by then settled in the requested state, has the court of that state a discretion nonetheless to order the return of the child? The House of Lords held that it had, having considered the law as stated in Australia, particularly, Scotland and New Zealand, and commented:

> This is as far as the comparative researches of counsel have taken us. It would be putting it too high to say that there is a strong tide of international judicial opinion in favour of a discretion in settlement cases. On the other hand, Kay J in Australia and Singer J in England are the only judges to have expressed a contrary view.[18]

All these cases contain a full, and predominant, consideration of domestic authority, as our rules of precedent require. But the courts approach the 1985 Act and the Convention scheduled to it not as if these were purely British measures but conscious of a duty to collaborate with other states party to the Convention in giving it an interpretation which, so far as possible, reflects

---

[16] *In re D (A Child) (Abduction: Rights of Custody)* [2006] UKHL 51, [2007] 1 AC 619.

[17] *Re H*, n. 12 above.

[18] *Re M (Children) (Abduction: Rights of Custody)* [2007] UKHL 55, [2008] AC 1288, para. 27.

their common intention. The underlying rationale of the Convention is of course that states should do as they would be done by. An English judge, asked to order the return of a child to what may be thought a less attractive country overseas, may be very sympathetic to the child; but the price of failing to order return in a case where the Convention requires it may of course be that return of a British child, abducted from Britain and taken to such a country, will not be ordered either. If, as has been said, the Convention is widely regarded as a great success, this is because, despite wide differences between the cultures and legal systems of the contracting states, '[a]ll are prepared to accept these differences for the sake of the reciprocal benefits which membership can bring'.[19]

In the cases so far touched on, our domestic courts have had the task of applying a convention given effect in this country by statute. But sometimes there is no statute giving full and formal effect to a convention which the UK has ratified. The 1951 Geneva convention relating to the Status of Refugees and its 1967 Protocol provide an example. The UK is one of about 140 states to have ratified these instruments, but they are scheduled to no statute. It has, however, been correctly said that 'the effect of successive legislative references and the content of the rules adopted for implementation of immigration and asylum law have led the courts to conclude that to all intents and purposes, they are indeed now part of domestic law'.[20] Once again, in this immensely important field, we can

---

[19] *In re J*, n. 14 above, para. 21.

[20] G. Goodwin-Gill and J. McAdam, *The Refugee in International Law* (3rd edn, Oxford University Press, 2007), 44; and see *R* v. *Secretary of State for the Home Department, Ex p. Sivakumaran* [1988] AC 958, 990;

see the British courts striving to give effect to the international consensus which the Convention expresses. The benign purpose of the Convention is obvious: to ensure that those fleeing from persecution in their home countries may take refuge in another country they enter or seek to enter, without being subject to penalty or the risk of being sent back to their home countries. But countries do not on the whole welcome refugees. So it is not surprising that application of the Convention has given rise to many difficult questions of interpretation.

Central to the Convention is its definition of a 'refugee' for Convention purposes as, to quote the words most often invoked, a person who,

> owing to well-founded fear of being persecuted for reasons of race, religion, nationality, membership of a particular social group or political opinion, is outside the country of his nationality and is unable, or owing to such fear, is unwilling to avail himself of the protection of that country.[21]

When can it be said that persecution is for reasons of membership of a particular social group? The House of Lords had to consider this in a case where two married Pakistani women had been forced to leave their homes and feared that, if they were returned to Pakistan, they would be at risk of being falsely accused of adultery, which could lead to extreme social consequences and the risk of being flogged or stoned to death.

R (European Roma Rights Centre) v. Immigration Officer at Prague Airport (United Nations High Commissioner for Refugees intervening) [2004] UKHL 55, [2005] 2 AC 1, para. 7.

[21] Article 1A(2).

They claimed asylum here.[22] It was accepted that they had a well-founded fear of persecution if returned to Pakistan,[23] but would the persecution be for reasons of their membership of a particular social group and, if so, what was that group? Following an Australian decision,[24] it had become accepted that a particular social group had to exist independently of the persecution. A majority of the House held that the applicants were members of a particular social group consisting either of women in Pakistan, who were disadvantageously treated and received no protection by the state, or of women suspected of adultery and receiving no protection by the state. In reaching this view, which differed from that of the Court of Appeal,[25] the House paid close attention to cases decided in Australia, Canada and the United States, and also to an impressive New Zealand judgment drawing on the case law and practice in Germany, The Netherlands, Sweden, Denmark, Canada, Australia and the United States.[26] A few years later the House had to revisit the question, this time in the case of a girl who, after a traumatic history, arrived here from Sierra Leone aged fifteen and claimed asylum on the basis that, if returned to Sierra Leone, she would be at risk of subjection to female genital mutilation ('FGM'), a practice prevalent in that country.[27] It

---

[22] *R v. Immigration Appeal Tribunal, Ex p. Shah* [1999] 2 AC 629.
[23] *Ibid.* at 639 E.
[24] *Applicant A v. Minister for Immigration and Ethnic Affairs* (1997) 71 ALJR 381, 401.
[25] [1998] 1 WLR 74.
[26] [1999] 2 AC 629, at 643 D.
[27] *Fornah v. Secretary of State for the Home Department* [2006] UKHL 46, [2007] 1 AC 412.

was common ground in the appeal that FGM constituted treatment which would amount to persecution within the meaning of the Convention and that, if the applicant were, as she contended, a member of a particular social group, the persecution would be for reasons of her membership.[28] So the issue was a narrow one. But this time the House was unanimous in allowing her appeal against an adverse decision of the Court of Appeal, holding that the particular social group to which she belonged was either all women in Sierra Leone or indigenous Sierra Leonean women who had not undergone FGM. The House was of course assisted by the earlier decision just described, but also reviewed the case law of the United States, Australia, Canada, New Zealand and Austria. I observed:

> It is well established that the Convention must be interpreted in accordance with its broad humanitarian objective and having regard to the principles, expressed in the preamble, that human beings should enjoy the widest possible exercise of these rights and freedoms. Since the Convention is an international instrument which no supra-national court has the ultimate authority to interpret, the construction put upon it by other states, while not determinative … is of importance, and in case of doubt articles 31–33 of the Vienna Convention on the Law of Treaties (1980) (Cmnd 7964) may be invoked to aid the process of interpretation.[29]

It is no doubt inevitable, where an international instrument like the Refugee Convention falls to be interpreted in different

---

[28] *Ibid.* at para. 25.
[29] *Ibid.* at para. 10.

countries by different national courts, that differences of interpretation arise. Such was notably the case in relation to an important question: for purposes of the Convention, must the persecution of which an applicant has a well-founded fear be by the foreign state or its agents, or is it enough that the persecution is by non-state agents against whom the foreign state offers inadequate protection? In this country, the view was taken that persecution by non-state agents, if the state gave inadequate protection, was enough,[30] a view shared by a majority of European state parties and the United States, Canada and Australia.[31] But it was clear that both France and Germany supported the first answer.[32] So the House was obliged to consider whether there was a single autonomous meaning of Article 1A(2). Having referred to the principles applicable to interpretation of an international convention,[33] the House concluded that there was a single correct autonomous meaning, which was that favoured by the majority of states.[34]

What if a person has a well-founded fear of persecution in one part of his home country and is unable to avail himself of the protection of his country in that part, but has no such fear and no such inability in another part? Is he entitled to recognition as a refugee in another country to which he

---

[30] *Adan v. Secretary of State for the Home Department* [1999] 1 AC 293, 305–6; *Horvath v. Secretary of State for the Home Department* [2001] 1 AC 489.

[31] *R v. Secretary of State for the Home Department, Ex p. Adan* [2001] 2 AC 477, 491, 519.

[32] *Ibid.* at 491–2, 508–10, 512.

[33] *Ibid.* at 515–18.

[34] *Ibid.* at 518–20.

flees? These are questions which the parties to the Convention did not expressly address, but they were questions which were bound to arise, and did. Guidance was given by the Office of the United Nations High Commissioner for Refugees in its 1979 *Handbook* and a joint position adopted by the Council of the European Union in 1996. In the following year, the Court of Appeal accepted this joint position as reflecting a contemporary understanding of Convention obligations shared not only by the member states of the European Union but also, as shown by leading authorities in those countries, by Canada and Australia.[35] The test was whether, in all the circumstances, it was reasonable to expect the applicant for asylum to have moved to the part of his home country in which he had no well-founded fear of persecution. The question was posed: 'Would it be unduly harsh to expect this person who is being persecuted in one part of his country to move to another less hostile part of the country before seeking refugee status abroad?'[36]

That sounds like a workable test, however difficult to apply in practice, but it gave rise to differences of interpretation. In judging whether it would be unduly harsh to expect an asylum applicant to relocate to another part of his own country, should the comparison be made between conditions in his place of habitual residence and those in the place of putative relocation or with those in the country of intended asylum? And was the condition met if conditions in the place of puta-

35 *R v. Secretary of State for the Home Department, Ex p. Robinson* [1998] QB 929, 938–9.
36 *Thirunavukkarasu v. Canada (Minister of Employment and Immigration)* (1993) 109 DLR (4th) 682, 687.

tive relocation did not provide the applicant with the basic norms of civil, political and socio-economic rights? The Court of Appeal, following Canadian authority and rejecting a contrary view taken, with strong academic support, in New Zealand, held that the comparison had to be made with the place of putative relocation, and that it was not relevant whether the applicant would enjoy the basic norms of civil, political and socio-economic rights.[37] The Court of Appeal's rejection of the New Zealand approach was later endorsed by the House of Lords which, having reviewed the international case law and literature, found no consensus of expert international opinion.[38] But it preferred the Court of Appeal's approach to the rule followed in New Zealand for five reasons. First, there was nothing in the Convention from which the New Zealand interpretation could be derived. Secondly, acceptance of that rule could not be implied into the Convention since the thrust of the Convention was to ensure the fair and equal treatment of refugees in countries of asylum and was not directed (persecution apart) to the level of rights prevailing in the country of nationality. Thirdly, the New Zealand rule was not that expressed in a recent European Council Directive, which could not lay down a standard lower than the Convention required. Fourthly, the rule was not currently supported by such uniformity of international practice based on legal obligation and such consensus of professional and academic opinion as would be necessary to establish a rule of customary international law. And fifthly,

37 *E v. Secretary of State for the Home Department* [2003] EWCA Civ. 1032, [2004] QB 531.
38 *Januzi v. Secretary of State for the Home Department* [2006] UKHL 5, [2006] 2 AC 426, para. 14.

adoption of the rule would have anomalous consequences: it would mean, for a person persecuted in a poor country, that the accident of persecution would enable him to escape not only from the persecution but also from the poverty and destitution prevalent in his home country.[39] I refer to this history not to commend the correctness of the House of Lords' eventual decision, about which views may no doubt vary, but to illustrate the way in which courts across the world, grappling with the same problem arising under an international convention, seek, collaboratively, to feel their way towards a consensual international solution.

In the cases so far discussed, the issues of international law arose for decision in the English court in a straightforward and uncomplicated manner. This need not be so, and it was not so in *Jones v. Ministry of the Interior of the Kingdom of Saudi Arabia*[40] and its companion case.[41] In those cases the claimants sued Saudi Arabian entities and officials in England to recover damages for torture inflicted on them by the officials while the claimants were in prison in Saudi Arabia. The Saudi defendants resisted the claims, pleading that they were immune from the jurisdiction of the English court. The claimants faced an initial problem. Following a series of court decisions,[42] the UK had in the State Immunity Act 1978 legislated to bring our law of sovereign immunity into line with that of most other countries. The Act provided that a state and its departments

[39] *Ibid.* at paras. 15–19.

[40] [2006] UKHL 26, [2007] 1 AC 270.

[41] *Mitchell v. Al-Dali, ibid.*

[42] Notably, *The Philippine Admiral* [1977] AC 373; *Trendtex Trading Corporation v. Central Bank of Nigeria* [1977] QB 529.

were immune from the jurisdiction of the UK courts except as specifically provided in the Act. The claimants' problem was that, as all agreed, their claim did not come within any of the statutory exceptions, and a formidable body of authority from all over the world (including a United Nations Convention on Jurisdictional Immunities of States and Their Property, adopted by the General Assembly in December 2004 but not yet in force and not ratified by the UK) treated the immunity of states as extending also to their agents acting in an official capacity.[43]

To overcome this problem, the claimants advanced three arguments. The first was that the issue of immunity engaged Article 6 of the European Convention on Human Rights, given effect by the Human Rights Act 1998, in its guarantee of a right of access to the court. To support this, the claimants relied on a decision of the European Court of Human Rights[44] which the House of Lords found unpersuasive but grudgingly accepted.[45] Crucial to the claimants' case was their second argument. This was that the grant of immunity to the Kingdom of Saudi Arabia on behalf of itself or its servants would be inconsistent with a peremptory norm of international law, a rule superior in effect to other rules of international law (in the legal vernacular, a *jus cogens* applicable *erga omnes*) which requires that the practice of torture should be suppressed and the victims of torture compensated.[46] Or, as the argument was summarised by Lord Hoffmann,

---

[43] *Jones*, paras. 7–10.

[44] *Al-Adsani* v. *United Kingdom* (2001) 34 EHRR 273.

[45] *Jones*, paras. 14, 64, 103–5.

[46] *Ibid.* at para. 14.

> although the right [of access to a court] is not absolute and
> its infringement by state immunity is ordinarily justified
> by mandatory rules of international law, no immunity
> is required in cases of torture. That is because the
> prohibition of torture is a peremptory norm or jus cogens
> which takes precedence over other rules of international
> law, including the rules of state immunity.[47]

In advancing this argument, the claimants were of course able
to rely on the revulsion against torture felt by any ordinarily
humane person and by an instinctive feeling that victims of
torture should be compensated. But, as was pointed out by
Lord Hoffmann in his opinion,

> It is not for a national court to 'develop' international
> law by unilaterally adopting a version of that law which,
> however desirable, forward-looking and reflective of
> values it may be, is simply not accepted by other states.[48]

So, when the case reached the House of Lords in the spring of
2006, the House had no choice but to try to decide how international law then stood.

Central to the claimants' argument was the 1984
UN Convention against Torture and other Cruel, Inhuman
or Degrading Treatment or Punishment,[49] to which the UK
and Saudi Arabia and most other states were parties. It was
common ground that the proscription of torture in the Torture Convention had, in international law, the superior status

---

[47] *Ibid.* at para. 39.
[48] *Ibid.* at para. 63. See also para. 34.
[49] (1990) (Cm 1775).

which the claimants ascribed to it.[50] But did it entitle or require contracting states such as the UK to entertain civil claims for damages for torture inflicted by a foreign sovereign state and its agents abroad?[51]

In arguing that it did, their third argument, the claimants relied on a wide range of materials, including the reasoning of the minority of the Grand Chamber of the European Court of Human Rights in a case arising on very similar facts;[52] observations by the members of the House of Lords in the first and third Pinochet appeals;[53] a number of decisions made in the United States; a decision of the International Tribunal for the Former Yugoslavia;[54] a decision of the Italian Court of Cassation;[55] and a recommendation made to Canada by the UN Committee against Torture in July 2005. These materials were considered in some detail in the opinions of the House but were, for a variety of reasons, largely discounted.[56] More telling were four principal arguments the other way. First, a recent decision of the International Court of Justice upheld a claim for immunity by

---

[50] *Jones*, paras. 15, 43.

[51] It has been pointed out that no consideration was given to whether, if the English court had jurisdiction, the claimants could show a cause of action sounding in tort: see Hazel Fox, *The Law of State Immunity* (2nd edn, Oxford University Press, 2008), 165–6.

[52] *Al-Adsani* v. *United Kingdom*, n. 44 above.

[53] *R* v. *Bow Street Metropolitan Stipendiary Magistrate, Ex p. Pinochet Ugarte* (No. 1) [2000] 1 AC 61 and (No. 3) [2000] 1 AC 147.

[54] *Prosecutor* v. *Furunzija* (1998) 38 ILM 317.

[55] *Ferrini* v. *Federal Republic of Germany* (2004) Cass sez un 5044/04; 87 *Rivista di Diretto Internazionale* 539.

[56] *Jones*, paras. 18–23, 40–5, 49, 51–8, 63, 95–9.

a serving foreign minister whose arrest was sought by Belgium, by virtue of his office, even though he was accused of crimes against humanity, a charge subject to the same level of proscription in international law as that against torture.[57] Secondly, while the Torture Convention contained detailed provisions governing the assumption and exercise of criminal jurisdiction, it did not provide for universal civil jurisdiction, requiring a civil right of action only where the torture had been committed in territory under the jurisdiction of a forum state.[58] Thirdly, the 2004 UN Convention on Immunity, which despite its status as work in progress represented the clearest and most comprehensive statement of international legal opinion on the subject, provided no exception from immunity where claims were made based on acts of torture.[59] And fourthly, there was no evidence that states had recognised or given effect to an international law obligation to exercise universal jurisdiction over claims arising from alleged breaches of peremptory norms of international law, and there was no consensus of judicial and learned opinion that they should: thus the rule on immunity was well understood and accepted and there was no generally accepted exception from it.[60] These conclusions meant that, even if Article 6 of the European Convention was engaged, denial of jurisdiction to entertain the claimants' claims involved no denial of their right of access to a

---

[57] *Congo, Democratic Republic of v. Belgium (Case concerning arrest warrant of 11 April 2000)* [2002] ICJ Rep 3. See *Jones*, paras. 24, 48–9.

[58] *Jones*, paras. 25, 46.

[59] *Ibid.* at paras. 8, 26, 47.

[60] *Ibid.* at paras. 26, 27, 50.

court. In any event, it was not considered possible to read an exception into the State Immunity Act 1978 under Section 3 of the Human Rights Act.[61]

The outcome of this case is one that many regret, quite apart from the claimants, and it may well be, as pointed out in the House, that the claimants' contention will come to represent the law of nations.[62] My point, however, is not to justify the decision: it is to point out, again, that the English court was not in this case expounding and applying a body of English law but was acting, to all intents and purposes, as a tribunal exploring and seeking to expound the law which prevails internationally.

As my final example I choose a case in which, as Lord Rodger put it, the House of Lords, 'a domestic court, finds itself deep inside the realm of international law – indeed inside the very chamber of the United Nations Security Council itself': *R (Al-Jedda)* v. *Secretary of State for Defence (JUSTICE and another intervening)*.[63] Mr Al-Jedda, a British resident and a national of the UK and Iraq, went to Iraq in September 2004 and was arrested by British forces the following month on the ground that he was involved in serious terrorism. This he denied, but the facts were not investigated in the legal proceedings and were assumed to be true for purposes of the legal argument. After arrest he was held for three years in a British detention facility in Iraq, without charge or trial. He applied for judicial review, contending that his right to personal freedom,

---

[61] *Ibid.* at paras. 35, 64, 103–5.
[62] *Ibid.* at para. 26.
[63] [2007] UKHL 58, [2008] AC 332, para. 55.

guaranteed by Article 5 of the European Convention and given effect by the Human Rights Act 1998, had been infringed.

It was claimed that Mr Al-Jedda was subject to British jurisdiction when held in the detention facility, he was clearly deprived of his liberty, and his detention did not fall within any of the specified exceptions to the Article 5 guarantee. He had, therefore, an unanswerable complaint unless, as the Secretary of State contended, his detention was required or permitted by a resolution of the UN Security Council which overrode the UK's international obligation as a party to the European Convention. In the Queen's Bench Divisional Court and in the Court of Appeal, this was the main issue between the parties, and it was decided against Mr Al-Jedda. It was reargued in the House of Lords with the same outcome. Security Council Resolution 1546, applicable to Iraq, was read as imposing an obligation to detain where this was necessary for imperative reasons of security, and effect was given to Article 103 of the United Nations Charter:

> In the event of a conflict between the obligations of the
> Members of the United Nations under the present Charter
> and their obligations under any other international
> agreement, their obligations under the present Charter
> shall prevail.

This was a ruling of some importance in international law. Mindful of the United Nations' commitment to human rights, the House of Lords did, however, emphasise that Mr Al-Jedda's rights under Article 5 should not be infringed to any extent greater than was inherent in his detention. It is a matter of history that, within days of the judgment, he was released.[64]

In the House of Lords, however, an even more important point arose. After the Court of Appeal had given judgment, the European Court of Human Rights made an admissibility decision in two conjoined applications, *Behrami* v. *France; Saramati* v. *France, Germany and Norway*.[65] These applications arose from events in Kosovo. *Behrami* concerned two children, one killed and one blinded by a cluster bomb which had been dropped by NATO forces and not cleared. *Saramati*, more analogous with *Al-Jedda*, concerned a man arrested and detained without charge or trial. They both blamed KFOR, an international security presence established under the auspices of the United Nations. The applicants' applications to the European Court raised essentially the same questions as I have already noted in *Al-Jedda*: were the applicants subject to the jurisdiction of the respondent states (Saramati withdrew his claim against Germany)? Were their Convention rights respectively violated? Were such violations required by UN Security Council Resolution 1244 applicable to Kosovo? But the European Court addressed a different issue: whether the conduct complained of was attributable to the respondent states or, instead, to the United Nations. Having considered the principles governing the responsibility of international organisations and identified a test of effective control, the Court concluded that a United Nations agency (UNMIK) was responsible for failing to clear the bomb, that the UN had

---

[64] *Ibid.* at paras. 39, 126–9, 136, 152.
[65] (2007) 45 EHRR SE 85.

effective control of KFOR, and that in each case the conduct complained of was attributable to the UN and so outside the European Convention. The Secretary of State welcomed this decision as manna from heaven, although it was not a result for which the UK, intervening in the case in Strasbourg, had contended. But he took the opportunity to argue in the House of Lords that the situation in Iraq was legally indistinguishable from that in Kosovo; therefore the same result should follow: the arrest and detention of Mr Al-Jedda were attributable to the UN and not the UK. For Mr Al-Jedda it was argued not that the *Behrami/Saramati* decision was wrong, but that the situation in Iraq was legally different from that in Kosovo.

The Secretary of State's argument was accepted in a carefully reasoned opinion of Lord Rodger,[66] and Lord Brown, although initially (if hesitantly) inclined to reject it,[67] ended by nailing his colours to the fence.[68] A majority rejected it. I went so far as to say that, in my opinion, the analogy with the situation in Kosovo broke down at almost every point,[69] a view with which Lady Hale and Lord Carswell agreed.[70] Eminent counsel in the case did not contend that *Behrami/Saramati* had been wrongly decided: the issue was how it should be applied and whether it could be distinguished.

Since the House of Lords' judgment, the correctness of the decision has been questioned, not least in an article whose purport is conveyed by its title: 'As Bad As It Gets: The

---

[66] [2007] UKHL 58, [2008] AC 332, paras. 57–113.
[67] *Ibid.* at para. 149.
[68] *Ibid.* at para. 156.
[69] *Ibid.* at para. 24.
[70] *Ibid.* at paras. 124, 131.

European Court's Behrami and Saramati Decision and General International Law'.[71] In this article my grounds for distinguishing *Behrami/Saramati* are not found to be 'particularly persuasive'[72] and the authors share Lord Rodger's view that the decision cannot really be distinguished from *Al-Jedda*. But they criticise the European Court's analysis as 'entirely at odds with the established rules of responsibility in international law',[73] 'wrong as a matter of law'[74] and leading to 'unacceptable results as a matter of policy'.[75] They also support the conclusion at which the House of Lords majority, even if for the wrong reasons, arrived:

> Unfortunately for the Government, when translated to the context of Iraq, *Behrami* [and *Saramati*] seemed even more absurd than it does in relation to Kosovo. Was the House of Lords truly supposed to say that all the actions of the US and UK troops in Iraq were attributable to the UN? As Lord Bingham himself noted, up until then nobody claimed that the UN was responsible for the Abu Ghraib torture scandal. Moreover, if we recall that the legal basis that the US and the UK relied on in the first place was implied authorization by the Security Council the logical consequence of the UK Government's reliance on *Behrami* [and *Saramati*] is that the *entire war and occupation*, all of it, was attributable to the UN. Faced with such a prospect,

71 Marko Milanovic and Tatjana Papic, *International and Comparative Law Quarterly* 58 (2009) 267–96.

72 *Ibid.* at 291.

73 *Ibid.* at 292.

74 *Ibid.* at 267.

75 *Ibid.* at 289.

> it is hardly surprising that the House was not going to
> follow *Behrami* [and *Saramati*].[76]

The authors' criticisms may or may not be justified. The controversy will doubtless rumble on. I shall not attempt to resolve it. My concern is not whether the House of Lords majority in *Al-Jedda*, or the European Court in *Behrami/Saramati*, was right or wrong. I dwell on *Al-Jedda* as a case study because, as I suggest, it highlights three points which are, together, the theme of this chapter. First, significant questions of international law, with a direct bearing on the lives, liberties and fortunes of individuals, fall to be decided in national courts. Secondly, this duty of decision is one that national courts cannot escape or evade, even if they would wish to do so. National courts cannot, of course, deploy the diversity of professional background, experience, learning and tradition which supranational courts can contribute to the resolution of international legal problems, but when such problems are raised by litigants in a national forum the court must decide them as best it can. And thirdly, this is not a function to be regretted. If we believe, as we probably do, that peace and good order in the world depend to a large extent on the observance of legal rules, on the international as on the national plane, the contribution made by national courts, not least our own, is one of which we – and, I hope, Miss Hamlyn – may be proud.

[76] *Ibid.* at 290.

3

Nonsense on international stilts?

We cannot doubt that Miss Hamlyn would have been intensely proud of the liberties and protections afforded by our domestic law, common law and statute, to those living in these islands. But it seems unlikely that the expression 'human rights' would ever have crossed her lips, or that the concept loomed at all largely in her consciousness. To the extent that it did, she would have thought in purely national terms. Magna Carta and the Petition of Right 1628, after all, important though they were, had no extra-territorial application, and were in any event more concerned to constrain the power of the Crown than confer rights on individuals. The French Declaration of the Rights of Man and the Citizen 1789 and the United States Bill of Rights 1791 certainly did have the object of conferring rights on individuals, but they too had no extra-territorial application. Miss Hamlyn's outlook was largely shared by her first lecturer, Sir Alfred Denning (as he then styled himself), in his justly celebrated 1949 lectures *Freedom under the Law* (which, amazingly as it now seems, earned him a rebuke by the Lord Chancellor of the day for exceeding the bounds of judicial reticence). Lord Justice Denning did, it is true, acknowledge that in some respects the French system of administrative law afforded the citizen better protection than our own system,[1] but he was doubtful

---

[1] *Freedom under the Law* (London: Stevens, 1949), 78.

if this system would suit us here.[2] In the main he referred to foreign systems in order, as Miss Hamlyn would have wished, to highlight the advantages which British citizens enjoyed under our own law. If he addressed the substance, he did not use the language, of human rights, let alone the international language of human rights.

It was in 1948, with the Universal Declaration of Human Rights, that human rights went global. The importance of the Universal Declaration is easy to underestimate, partly because it lacked any means of enforcement, partly because some of its articles were somewhat lame; Professor Sir Hersch Lauterpacht described Article 14, on asylum, as 'artificial to the point of flippancy'.[3] But these drawbacks should not blind us to the momentous implications of the Declaration: the adoption by the General Assembly of the newly formed United Nations, with forty-eight votes in favour, eight abstentions and no votes against, of a common standard of rights to be universally observed and secured. From this visionary initiative the modern, international, law of human rights has sprung. Its first fruit was the American Declaration of the Rights and Duties of Man 1948, but its most fertile offspring was the European Convention on Human Rights, just under two years younger, which referred to the Universal Declaration in its first recital.

When the European Convention was negotiated, British policy favoured the international protection of human rights, and the UK pressed for the right of a member state

---

[2] *Ibid.* 80.
[3] 'The Universal Declaration of Human Rights', *British Yearbook of International Law* 25 (1948) 354, 378–84.

(now found in Article 56) to extend its provisions to 'all or any of the territories for whose international relations it is responsible' – namely the colonial empire – although the provisions were to be applied in such territories 'with due regard ... to local requirements'. The UK promptly extended the Convention to forty-two territories, including the Channel Islands and the Isle of Man, but excluding a handful of territories of which the most significant were Southern Rhodesia, Hong Kong and Aden.[4] During the 1950s and 1960s many of these territories became independent and in the constitutions granted to them it became standard practice to include a chapter setting out the human rights which were, under this new constitutional dispensation, to receive constitutional protection. These chapters were closely modelled on the European Convention, but a number of these newly independent states chose to retain a right of appeal to the Judicial Committee of the Privy Council in Downing Street. Thus it transpired that the first exposure of British judges to the international law of human rights occurred in the Privy Council when the judges were called on to interpret constitutional provisions which, unlike the same provisions in the UK, formed part – and a very important part – of the domestic law of these countries. As was pointed out by Professor Andrew Harding in 2003,

> it is nonsense to say that British judges are [now] for
> the first time having to interpret a bill of rights. They
> have been doing this for years, and the case law is always
> relevant and often very helpful in terms of giving doctrinal

---

[4] A. W. Brian Simpson, *Human Rights and the End of Empire* (Oxford University Press, 2001), 838–9.

support to a bill of rights: indeed the Privy Council has more *comparative* experience in this respect than any court in the world.[5]

The Privy Council responded to the human rights chapters of ex-colonial constitutions with two voices, one traditional or conservative, the other broader and more internationalist in outlook. Reflective of the initial, conservative, approach was the statement of Lord Devlin in 1967 in *Director of Public Prosecutions* v. *Nasralla*, referring to Chapter III of the Jamaican Constitution, entitled 'Fundamental Rights and Freedoms', when he said:

> This chapter, as their Lordships have already noted, proceeds upon the presumption that the fundamental rights which it covers are already secured to the people of Jamaica by existing law. The laws in force are not to be subjected to scrutiny in order to see whether or not they conform to the precise terms of the protective provisions. The object of these provisions is to ensure that no future enactments shall in any matter which the chapter covers derogate from the rights which at the coming into force of the Constitution the individual enjoyed.[6]

This statement was cited and endorsed in later Privy Council cases.[7] Thus on this approach the chapter offered protection

---

[5] 'Comparative Case Law in Human Rights Cases in the Commonwealth: The Emerging Common Law of Human Rights' in *Judicial Comparativism in Human Rights Cases*, ed. E. Örücü (London: United Kingdom National Committee of Comparative Law, 2003), 183–200, at 187.

[6] [1967] 2 AC 238, 247–8.

[7] Among them, *de Freitas* v. *Benny* [1976] AC 239, 247, and *Maharaj* v. *Attorney-General of Trinidad and Tobago (No. 2)* [1979] AC 385, 395.

against erosion of rights enjoyed when the Constitution was adopted, but nothing would be a violation which would not at that time have been held to be such. So there could be no development of constitutionally protected human rights: they would remain for ever what they were in domestic law at a given moment of time, preserved for ever, like the buildings of Pompeii.

The alternative, and more internationalist, approach was that famously articulated by Lord Wilberforce in *Minister of Home Affairs* v. *Fisher*, again in the Privy Council, when, having referred to the European Convention and the Universal Declaration, he observed that

> These antecedents, and the form of Chapter I [of the Bermuda Constitution] itself, call for a generous interpretation avoiding what has been called 'the austerity of tabulated legalism', suitable to give to individuals the full measure of the fundamental rights and freedoms referred to.[8]

He continued:

> A Constitution is a legal instrument giving rise, amongst other things, to individual rights capable of enforcement in a court of law. Respect must be paid to the language which has been used and to the traditions and usages which have given meaning to that language. It is quite consistent with this, and with the recognition that rules of interpretation may apply, to take as a point of departure

---

[8] [1980] AC 319, 328. Lord Wilberforce's unattributed quotation is from de Smith, *The New Commonwealth and its Constitutions* (London: Stevens, 1964), 194.

> for the process of interpretation a recognition of the character and origin of the instrument, and to be guided by the principle of giving full recognition and effect to those fundamental rights and freedoms with a statement of which the Constitution commences.[9]

The tension between these approaches is revealingly illustrated by considering a particular problem. The Constitution of Jamaica, following the effect if not the precise wording of the British and American Bills of Rights, the Universal Declaration, the European Convention and the International Covenant on Civil and Political Rights 1966, proscribed the infliction of inhuman or degrading punishment or other treatment, but went on to protect the infliction of any description of punishment which was lawful in Jamaica when the Constitution took effect. There was no doubt that, under the Constitution, the death penalty was lawful, but in *Riley* v. *Attorney-General of Jamaica*[10] the question arose whether a prolonged delay between imposition of the death sentence and execution, the prisoner meanwhile being held on Death Row waiting to be hanged, could in itself amount to inhuman or degrading punishment or other treatment. The five-member Privy Council was divided. The judgment of the three-member majority was brief. It referred to Lord Devlin's statement in *Nasralla*, and other cases in which that statement had been repeated, and held that since a long delay in implementing a sentence of death lawfully imposed could not have been questioned before independence it could not be questioned under the

---

[9] [1980] AC, at 329.
[10] [1983] 1 AC 719.

Constitution either. Lord Scarman and Lord Brightman delivered a joint dissenting judgment. They based their approach on the principles adumbrated by Lord Wilberforce in *Fisher*. Reference was made to an earlier Privy Council appeal in which a long delay between sentence and execution had been greatly deplored,[11] but the *Riley* minority did not confine itself to expressions of regret. Instead it reviewed the international case law, citing four instances out of many in which judges in other countries had recognised the inhumanity and degradation which long-delayed implementation of the death penalty could cause. Three of the cases cited were American, one Indian; and the decision of the European Court of Human Rights in *Tyrer* v. *United Kingdom*,[12] where there were several weeks' delay in carrying out a Manx sentence of birching, was referred to. The minority therefore concluded:

> It is no exaggeration, therefore, to say that the jurisprudence of the civilised world, much of which is derived from common law principles and the prohibition against cruel and unusual punishments in the English Bill of Rights, has recognised and acknowledged that prolonged delay in executing a sentence of death can make the punishment when it comes inhuman and degrading. As the Supreme Court of California commented in *People v Anderson*, it is cruel and has dehumanising effects. Sentence of death is one thing: sentence of death followed by lengthy imprisonment prior to execution is another.[13]

[11] *Abbott* v. *Attorney-General of Trinidad and Tobago* [1979] 1 WLR 1342, 1345.

[12] (1979–80) 2 EHRR 1.

[13] *Ibid.* at 734–5.

The narrow conservative view favoured by the majority in *Riley*, making no reference to international sources (which do not appear to have been cited in argument), might no doubt have been the end of the matter. But, perhaps predictably, the problem arose again, this time in *Pratt and another* v. *Attorney General for Jamaica*,[14] and an enlarged panel of seven judges was mounted to hear the appeal. The facts were extreme. The appellants had been in prison, under sentence of death, for about fourteen years. On three occasions the death warrant had been read to them and they had been removed to the death cells immediately adjacent to the gallows. On the third occasion, a stay had been granted consequent upon the initiation of the proceedings. In the unanimous judgment of the Privy Council, delivered by Lord Griffiths, an account was given of interventions by the Inter-American Commission on Human Rights, and also of the United Nations Human Rights Committee established under the International Covenant. Reference was made to earlier Privy Council cases, particularly *Riley*, and other authority supporting the view that it cannot be inhuman or degrading to allow a defendant every opportunity to resist execution, even if this leads to long delay, a point which had been acknowledged by the minority in *Riley*.[15] But reference was also made to strong contrary statements in Zimbabwe,[16] a series of cases in the Supreme Court of India[17] and acceptance by

---

[14] [1994] 2 AC 1.

[15] *Riley*, at 735–6.

[16] *Catholic Commission for Justice and Peace in Zimbabwe* v. *Attorney General*, 24 June 1993, per Gubbay CJ.

[17] *Vatheeswaran* v. *State of Tamil Nadu* [1983] 2 SCR 348, 353; *Sher Singh* v. *State of Punjab* [1983] 2 SCR 582; *Smt. Treveniben* v. *State of Gujarat* [1989] 1 SCJ 383, 410.

the European Court in *Soering* v. *United Kingdom*[18] that a long period of delay in executing a death sentence might amount to inhuman or degrading treatment or punishment. So the conclusion was reached, departing from *Riley*:

> a state that wishes to retain capital punishment must accept the responsibility of ensuring that execution follows as swiftly as practicable after sentence, allowing a reasonable time for appeal and consideration of reprieve. It is part of the human condition that a condemned man will take every opportunity to save his life through use of the appellate procedure. If the appellate procedure enables the prisoner to prolong the appellate hearings over a period of years, the fault is to be attributed to the appellate system that permits such delay and not to the prisoner who takes advantage of it. Appellate procedures that echo down the years are not compatible with capital punishment. The death row phenomenon must not become established as part of our jurisprudence.[19]

The effect of this judgment was to set a term of five years from the passing of a death sentence, after which the prisoner could not ordinarily be executed.[20] This ruling was very unwelcome to the authorities in a number of countries to which it applied, and was thought to encourage a move to establish a local Caribbean Court of Justice (CCJ) which could depart from the ruling. The CCJ was duly established, but in one of its early judgments it gave lengthy reasons for upholding the

---

[18] (1989) 11 EHRR 439.
[19] [1994] 2 AC, at 33.
[20] *Ibid.* at 35.

Privy Council's decision on delay in implementation of the death penalty.[21]

If human rights are to be meaningful and valuable to those whose rights they are, the decision in *Pratt* is greatly to be preferred, I would suggest, to that in *Riley*, and it was the adoption of a broad, internationalist, approach which led the Privy Council to that result. I would make the same claim for a trilogy of Privy Council decisions raising a different but related question. This was whether, accepting the death penalty itself to be lawful (because constitutionally protected), a mandatory requirement that sentence of death be passed on any person convicted of murder, or of a specified category of murder, without any forensic opportunity for mitigation and consideration of extenuating circumstances, was inhuman and degrading treatment or punishment. The point was first raised by two men convicted of murder in, respectively, St Lucia and St Vincent, each of whose criminal codes (following the British model) provided a mandatory death sentence for murder. They challenged, in the Privy Council, the compatibility of the mandatory death sentences passed upon them with the prohibition of inhuman or degrading treatment or punishment in the respective constitutions, and the Privy Council referred the question back to the Eastern Caribbean Court of Appeal. A majority of that court, in a ground-breaking judgment delivered by Sir Dennis Byron CJ, held that the mandatory death sentence was indeed incompatible in each case (although one of the appellants later succeeded in an appeal

---

[21] *Attorney General of Barbados v. Joseph and Boyce* (CCJ Appeal No CV 2 of 2005).

against conviction). The Crown appealed to the Privy Council against the majority ruling, with the support of attorneys general representing other Caribbean countries. Heard in succession were two other appeals, raising the same issue, by defendants convicted of murder and mandatorily sentenced to death in Belize and St Christopher and Nevis respectively. Thus the Privy Council heard appeals by the Crown in *R v. Hughes* (St Lucia)[22] and by the convicted defendants in *Reyes v. The Queen* (Belize)[23] and *Fox v. The Queen* (St Christopher and Nevis).[24]

In three unanimous judgments, the Privy Council upheld the conclusion reached by Sir Dennis Byron. The fullest judgment was given in *Reyes*, a case notable for the fact that the Attorney General of Belize declined to appear to support the mandatory death penalty, although that was specifically laid down in the law of Belize for certain categories of murder, including murder by shooting. Reyes had shot and killed a man and his wife. Whatever the position twenty years earlier in *Riley*, there was no shortage of citation in these three appeals. Counsel presented the Privy Council with a cornucopia of foreign authority. Thus in its judgment the Board was able to draw on the international instruments already mentioned,[25] the decisions of bodies such as the Inter-American Commission on Human Rights, the UN Human Rights Committee and the European Court of Human Rights,[26] and

---

[22] [2002] UKPC 12, [2002] 2 AC 259.
[23] [2002] UKPC 11, [2002] 2 AC 235.
[24] [2002] UKPC 13, [2002] 2 AC 284.
[25] *Reyes*, paras. 18–21.
[26] *Ibid.* at paras. 40–2.

the case law of India,[27] South Africa,[28] Guyana,[29] the United States,[30] Mauritius,[31] Canada,[32] Belize[33] and the Eastern Caribbean Court of Appeal.[34] The conclusion reached was that:

> the provision requiring sentence of death to be passed on the defendant on his conviction of murder by shooting subjected him to inhuman or degrading punishment or other treatment incompatible with his right under ... the Constitution in that it required sentence of death to be passed and precluded any judicial consideration of the humanity of sentencing him to death.[35]

The social evil caused by the misuse of firearms was recognised, but so was the difference between one crime and one offender and another. So it was held:

> To deny the offender the opportunity, before sentence is passed, to seek to persuade the court that in all the circumstances to condemn him to death would be disproportionate and inappropriate is to treat him as no human being should be treated and thus to deny his basic humanity, the core of the right which [this provision of the Constitution] exists to protect.[36]

---

[27] *Ibid.* at paras. 13, 14, 36.
[28] *Ibid.* at paras. 14, 26, 30.
[29] *Ibid.* at para. 15.
[30] *Ibid.* at paras. 26, 34, 36.
[31] *Ibid.* at para. 26.
[32] *Ibid.* at paras. 26, 30, 36.
[33] *Ibid.* at para. 30.
[34] *Ibid.* at para. 32.
[35] *Ibid.* at para. 43.
[36] *Ibid.*

This contrasts with a decision of the Privy Council in 1966, rejecting an appellant's argument that a mandatory death sentence imposed on him under the law of Rhodesia and Nyasaland was inconsistent with a constitutional prohibition of inhuman or degrading treatment or punishment.[37] In that case the Board discounted the relevance of American authority on grounds later held to be unsound and effectively abdicated its duty of constitutional adjudication.[38] When, on reference back by the Privy Council for re-sentencing, Reyes appeared before the Chief Justice of Belize, counsel for the Crown did not argue for imposition of the death penalty.[39]

In a later case, Lord Hoffmann described the Board's decision in *Reyes* as:

> heavily influenced by developments in international
> human rights law and the jurisprudence of a
> number of other countries, including states in the
> Caribbean.[40]

It has in its turn proved influential. When exactly the same issue concerning the constitutionality of a mandatory death

[37] *Runyowa* v. *The Queen* [1967] 1 AC 26.

[38] See the criticism of this decision in *Bowe* v. *The Queen* [2006] UKPC 10, [2006] 1 WLR 1623, para. 40: Crown counsel in that case declined to rely on *Runyowa*, which he described as 'barbaric' and offensive to a modern sense of justice.

[39] E. Fitzgerald and K. Starmer, *A Guide to Sentencing in Capital Cases* (London: Death Penalty Project, 2007), Appendix I, paras. 3, 29. In laying down guidelines for sentencing in such cases the Chief Justice also drew on foreign authority: para. 15.

[40] *Boyce* v. *The Queen* [2004] UKPC 32, [2005] 1 AC 400, para. 27.

penalty arose in the High Court of Malawi, the court was referred to *Reyes* and said in its judgment:

> The decision in *Reyes v The Queen*, while a judicial decision, is also a whole treatise on the prevailing common law jurisprudence on the constitutionality of the mandatory requirement of the death penalty; and we acknowledge that the decision in *Reyes v The Queen* has been a valuable leading source for us in reaching our own decision in the matter before us in which we are having to determine precisely the same issue.[41]

The court reached the same conclusion, as did the Constitutional Court and the Supreme Court of Uganda, again citing *Reyes*, when the same issue arose there.[42]

In a further trilogy of cases, opinion in the Privy Council was sharply and narrowly divided, and in two of the three cases savings clauses in the respective Constitutions were held to protect the mandatory death penalty which the law laid down as the penalty for murder.[43] But all members of the Board accepted that the mandatory death penalty constituted inhuman or degrading punishment or treatment, a fact accepted by Trinidad and Tobago while successfully defending

[41] *Kafantayeni and others* v. *Attorney General* (Constitutional Case No. 12 of 2005, 27 April 2007), per Singini, Kapanda and Kamwambe JJ.

[42] *Kigula and 416 others* v. *The Attorney General* (Constitutional Petition No. 6 of 2003, 10 June 2005), *Attorney General* v. *Kigula and 416 others* (Constitutional Appeal No. 03 of 2006, 21 January 2008).

[43] *Boyce* v. *The Queen* [2004] UKPC 32, [2005] 1 AC 400 (Barbados); *Matthew* v. *State of Trinidad and Tobago* [2004] UKPC 33, [2005] 1 AC 433 (Trinidad and Tobago); *Watson* v. *The Queen* [2004] UKPC 34, [2005] 1 AC 472 (Jamaica).

its constitutionality in reliance on a savings clause.[44] There was no such acceptance by Barbados, also successful in defending its mandatory death penalty. But on 3 May 2009 the Deputy Prime Minister and Attorney General of Barbados announced that his Government would be moving to abolish the mandatory nature of the penalty, while preserving the penalty itself. 'The mandatory death sentence', he said, 'can no longer be defended. The judge should have some power to determine what sentence should be imposed for a capital offence, with the benefit of a pre-sentencing report.' The Government also pledged to repeal the savings clause relied on to protect pre-independence legislation from constitutional challenge even if it contravened fundamental human rights guarantees. These changes would bring Barbados into line with the judgment of the Inter-American Court of Human Rights in *Boyce et al.* v. *Barbados*,[45] which Barbados had undertaken to observe.

From this account of Privy Council decision-making, certain points, I suggest, emerge. The initial reaction of British judges to interpretation of constitutionally protected human rights was cautious and hesitant. Foreign authority attracted little attention. This reaction was the product in part of professional habit, in part of unfamiliarity, in part perhaps of a belief that when it came to fundamental human rights Britain was the world's educator, not its pupil. But the legal culture changed. It came to be recognised that human rights, if truly fundamental, could not be demarcated by national boundaries. The experience and judgments of other countries confronting the

[44] See *Boyce*, paras. 27, 74; *Matthew*, paras. 6, 36; *Watson*, paras. 29, 35, 55.
[45] Judgment of 20 November 2007, Series C, No. 169.

same or similar problems could be relevant and influential. So instructed, the court was able to reach what I, at least, would regard as more just decisions, better reflecting the modern values of society. But the exercise I have been rather impressionistically describing was of course on a small scale, involving very few British judges. It cannot compare with the much more radical change which occurred on 2 October 2000 when the Human Rights Act 1998 gave effect to the main provisions of the European Convention and the whole British judiciary, from bottom to top, were all but required to administer the international law of human rights to which the Convention, through the decisions of the Strasbourg institutions and particularly the European Court of Human Rights, had given rise. Although the Act only required the courts to 'take into account' the Strasbourg jurisprudence,[46] it also made it unlawful for a public authority, including a court, to act incompatibly with a Convention right[47] and the British courts have generally taken the line – understandably and, as I think, rightly – that, where the European Court has expounded the meaning of a Convention article in a clear and consistent way, the British courts should ordinarily follow that lead in the absence of some good reason (such as changed circumstances, misunderstanding or unpersuasive reasoning) for not doing so.[48] So our judges found themselves, at a stroke (even if the stroke was delayed

---

[46] Section 2(1) of the Act.

[47] Section 6(1), (3)(a).

[48] *R (Alconbury Developments Ltd)* v. *Secretary of State for the Environment, Transport and the Regions* [2001] UKHL 23, [2003] 2 AC 295; *R* v. *Spear* [2002] UKHL 31, [2003] 1 AC 734; *R (Ullah)* v. *Special Adjudicator* [2004] UKHL 26, [2004] 2 AC 323.

from 9 November 1998 until 2 October 2000), called upon to administer an international code of human rights largely laid down by the European Court in Strasbourg.

Given the large British input into the text of the Convention and the general tradition of respect for individual rights in this country, it might have been thought that we should rarely, if ever, be held to have violated it. This, I think, was the expectation among the British draftsmen and negotiators of the Convention, at least so far as the United Kingdom itself was concerned. The reality proved to be otherwise. In their magisterial work, *The Law of Human Rights*,[49] Messrs Clayton and Tomlinson have identified over 150 cases up to the end of 2008 in which the European Court has found a violation by the UK.[50] While no violations have been found of some Articles (such as Articles 4 and 9), and very few of some other Articles (such as Articles 7, 11, 12 and 14 and Articles 1, 2 and 3 of the First Protocol), other Articles have given rise to more findings of violation: 28 of Article 5 (the right to security of the person), 39 of Article 6 (the right to a fair trial) and 45 of Article 8 (the right, qualified though it is, to respect for private and family life, home and correspondence). That Article 8 should have led to so many adverse findings is not perhaps surprising: the scope of the Article is not clearly defined by its very general language, and it covers a field in which the protection offered by English domestic law was piecemeal and in some respects inadequate. Most of these violations were found

---

[49] 2nd edn, Oxford University Press, 2009. I have drawn heavily on this invaluable book, to which I am much indebted.

[50] See *ibid.* at paras 7.106, 8.130, 10.263, 11.533, 11.509, 12.370, 13.197, 15.386, 16.120, 17.203, 18.145, 19.97, 20.49.

in cases where the events occurred before the 1998 Act and the British courts could not have applied the Convention; in only 3 or 4 of the 45 cases had the applicant, when seeking redress unsuccessfully in the domestic courts, been able to rely on the Act and the Convention. Brief consideration of some of these 45 cases throws an interesting and revealing light on how, in practice, the Convention has had effect. I shall touch on five classes of case leading to an adverse decision under Article 8, asking in relation to each whether the trend of decision-making at Strasbourg is to be welcomed and whether the Strasbourg outcome is one at which our domestic law would have arrived in any event.

The first class of case involves the interception of private communications, whether in a national[51] or an international[52] context, the interception of a message sent by pager,[53] or the placing of listening devices in houses[54] or the workplace[55] or a police station,[56] or a police cell[57] or a prison waiting area.[58] A complaint by two members of what was then called the National Council for Civil Liberties that they had been

[51] *Malone v. United Kingdom* (1984) 7 EHRR 14.
[52] *Liberty v. United Kingdom* (2009) 48 EHRR 1.
[53] *Taylor-Sabori v. United Kingdom* (2003) 36 EHRR 248.
[54] *Govell v. United Kingdom* (1999) EHRLR 121; *Armstrong v. United Kingdom* (2003) 36 EHRR 515; *Chalkley v. United Kingdom* (2003) 37 EHRR 680; *Lewis v. United Kingdom* (2004) 39 EHRR 213.
[55] *Hewitson v. United Kingdom* (2003) 37 EHRR 687; *Copland v. United Kingdom* (2007) 45 EHRR 858.
[56] *Khan v. United Kingdom* (2001) 31 EHRR 1016.
[57] *Wood v. United Kingdom*, Judgment of 16 November 2004; *Allan v. United Kingdom* (2003) 36 EHRR 143.
[58] *Allan v. United Kingdom*, n. 57 above.

placed under secret surveillance by the Security Service was found to be admissible, but was the subject of a friendly settlement and not of a final decision.[59] In all these cases the basis of the adverse decision was not that the recording activities in question were inherently objectionable and impermissible in any circumstances but that they involved an interference with the right protected by Article 8 and were not the subject of any legal regulatory framework and so were not in accordance with the law, as any official interference with an Article 8 right must be if it is to be justified. Following these adverse decisions, action was taken by the UK to make clear when and on what conditions activities such as these could be carried out.

Critics of the Strasbourg court might see this insistence on legal definition as a pedantic and rather bureaucratic preferment of form over substance. That is not a view I share. The rule of law, I would suggest, requires that, if a right recognised as fundamental is to be the subject of official interference, the circumstances, nature, extent and conditions of such interference should be clearly and publicly laid down by law. This enables the individual to know in advance when his or her rights may be lawfully infringed. It removes the element of arbitrariness necessarily inherent in a broad and ill-defined discretion. And it gives the individual a right of redress if his or her rights are infringed in circumstances where the law does not permit it.

Would the changes made in response to these adverse decisions have been made anyway? Perhaps, but it seems unlikely. The authorities themselves would have had little

---

[59] *Hewitt and Harman (No. 1)* v. *United Kingdom* (1991) 14 EHRR 657.

incentive to introduce changes which would, to some extent, restrict their freedom of action. The public tend to believe that those who are the object of hostile action by the authorities are probably up to no good, and have no cause for complaint if they have nothing to hide. The victims of intrusive surveillance would have little appeal to Parliament or the public. So it seems on the whole probable that, but for the Strasbourg decisions, official practice would have continued in this country very much as it had been.

A second, quite different, class of cases leading to adverse decisions under Article 8 concerns the right of the individual to know of material held on official files concerning him or her. This may arise from an individual's wish to know what is recorded in social service records concerning his or her early years and personal development.[60] Or it may concern official records containing information pertaining to an individual's exposure to radiation[61] or the effects of chemical weapons testing.[62] In one case an applicant's claim in Strasbourg succeeded not on the basis of denial of access to information held on official files but on the basis that the information should not have been retained by the police at all: the case related to fingerprints and DNA samples taken from an eleven-year-old boy who had been arrested and charged but acquitted at trial, and to fingerprints and DNA samples taken from a man arrested and charged but against whom the case had been discontinued.

---

[60] As in *Gaskin* v. *United Kingdom* (1989) 12 EHRR 36; *MG* v. *United Kingdom* (2003) 36 EHRR 22.

[61] *McGinley and Egan* v. *United Kingdom* (1998) 27 EHRR 1.

[62] *Roche* v. *United Kingdom* (2006) 42 EHRR 599.

The decision reached, adverse to the UK, was that the finger-prints and samples could not be retained.[63]

The Strasbourg cases do not hold that the individual has an unqualified right to know what information is held about him or her on official files. They accept that disclosure may be withheld where it would be injurious to the individual's health[64] or would infringe the rights of others.[65] Again, this trend of decision-making is, in my opinion, to be welcomed. It is trite, but it is also true, to observe that knowledge is power, and that an individual cannot correct what may be serious errors in an official dossier unless he/she knows of its content. But in a more fundamental sense this issue bears on the relationship between the individual and the state. If, as we would wish to suppose, the state is a construct established to serve our interests and not to become our master, it would seem obvious that, absent special circumstances (such as a current investigation or a threat to national security), we should be entitled to know personal information pertinent to our wellbeing. And it would seem right that the state should not continue to keep fingerprints and DNA samples taken from people who have been convicted of no crime when it was suspicion of committing such crime which justified the taking of the fingerprints and samples in the first place.

I question whether, left to its own devices, domestic law would have delivered even the qualified right to know recognised by the Convention. The English common law failed

---

[63] *S* v. *United Kingdom* (2009) 48 EHRR 1169, a decision of the Grand Chamber.

[64] *Martin* v. *United Kingdom* (1996) 21 EHRR CD 112.

[65] *Willsher* v. *United Kingdom* (1997) 23 EHRR CD 188.

to develop a coherent law of privacy;[66] the tradition of official secrecy in this country has always been strong; and courts have often yielded to the argument that any possibility of disclosure would adversely affect the quality of official records since those compiling them would (it is said) be less candid if their observations could ever be seen by the party to whom they refer. In relation to the retention of fingerprints and DNA samples taken from unconvicted suspects, one can be more certain because, in a case governed by the Human Rights Act, a Queen's Bench Divisional Court, the Court of Appeal and a unanimous House of Lords dismissed the challenge to retention.[67] One Law Lord expressed his concern as being 'simply to indicate how very clear a case this seems to me to be'. His problem was 'in discerning any coherent basis on which the challenge can still be sustained'.[68]

A third group of cases concerns the correspondence of serving prisoners. In an early case a violation by the UK was found where a prisoner's letters to his MP were stopped and he was refused permission to consult a solicitor.[69] In a later case the routine opening of a prisoner's letters to his solicitor was held to be a breach of Article 8.[70] A blanket denial of the right to vote in national elections to serving prisoners was

[66] *Kaye* v. *Robertson* [1991] FSR 62; *Wainwright* v. *Home Office* [2003] UKHL 53, [2004] 2 AC 406.

[67] *R (S)* v. *Chief Constable of South Yorkshire Police* [2002] EWHC 478 (Admin.), [2002] EWCA Civ. 1275, [2002] 1 WLR 3223, [2004] UKHL 39, [2004] 1 WLR 2196.

[68] [2004] UKHL 39, at para. 85.

[69] *Golder* v. *United Kingdom* (1975) 1 EHRR 524.

[70] *Campbell* v. *United Kingdom* (1992) 15 EHRR 137.

held to breach Article 3 of the First Protocol.[71] A blanket denial of facilities for artificial insemination to serving prisoners was similarly held to be disproportionate.[72]

Some of these decisions might have been reached by our domestic courts anyway, since the common law has robustly insisted on the privilege attaching to legal correspondence. Thus, a requirement that a prisoner be absent when his legal correspondence was examined by prison officers was found by the House of Lords to be unlawful at common law as well as a breach of Article 8.[73] Others among the decisions would, I think, have been very unlikely, since the courts would have lacked any principle upon which to base them.

A general culture of respect for the rights of prisoners may perhaps be seen as the hallmark of a civilised society. I was seeking to summarise the values of the common law and the Convention when, in 2001, I said, with the approval of my colleagues:

> Any custodial order inevitably curtails the enjoyment, by the person confined, of rights enjoyed by other citizens. He cannot move freely and choose his associates as they are entitled to do. It is indeed an important objective of such an order to curtail such rights, whether to punish him or protect other members of the public or both. But the order does not wholly deprive the person confined of all rights enjoyed by other citizens. Some rights, perhaps

[71] *Hirst* v. *United Kingdom (No. 2)* (2004) 38 EHRR 825, (2006) 42 EHRR 849.

[72] *Dickson* v. *United Kingdom* (2008) 46 EHRR 927, GC.

[73] *R (Daly)* v. *Secretary of State for the Home Department* [2001] UKHL 26, [2001] 2 AC 532.

in an attenuated or qualified form, survive the making of the order. And it may well be that the importance of such surviving rights is enhanced by the loss or partial loss of other rights. Among the rights which, in part at least, survive are three important rights, closely related but free standing, each of them calling for appropriate legal protection: the right of access to a court; the right of access to legal advice; and the right to communicate confidentially with a legal adviser under the seal of legal professional privilege. Such rights may be curtailed only by clear and express words, and then only to the extent reasonably necessary to meet the ends which justify the curtailment.[74]

A fourth group of Article 8 cases, worthy of brief mention, concerns the right to respect for one's home. This is not a right which, as such, the common law has recognised and, while it has been generally hostile towards unwarranted intrusions into premises which a person lawfully occupies, the Convention, as interpreted and applied in Strasbourg, has proved more so.[75] A domestic court applying national law would have been unlikely to have condemned, as the Strasbourg court did on Article 8 grounds, a refusal by the Guernsey authorities, because of a housing shortage, to allow the applicants to occupy a house which they owned on the island.[76] A more vexed question, not yet perhaps finally resolved, is whether the Article 8 right to respect for the home may be

[74] *Ibid.* at paras. 5, 24, 29, 34, 36.
[75] See *McLeod* v. *United Kingdom* (1998) 27 EHRR 493, *Keegan* v. *United Kingdom* (2007) 44 EHRR 716.
[76] *Gillow* v. *United Kingdom* (1986) 11 EHRR 335.

successfully relied on to resist eviction by a person whose right to occupy property in domestic law has ceased, whether because his right has expired or because it has been lawfully brought to an end by notice. In *Connors* v. *United Kingdom*,[77] where the applicant and his family had lived on a local authority gipsy site for most of the sixteen years preceding termination of his licence, the Strasbourg court held unanimously that Article 8 was applicable. More recently, in a case where a husband's right to occupy a local authority house had come to an end on his wife's termination of a joint tenancy, the outcome at Strasbourg, again reached unanimously, was the same. This case, *McCann v United Kingdom*,[78] fell within the Human Rights Act, but the husband's challenge failed in the domestic courts because of adverse House of Lords authority.[79] He succeeded in Strasbourg, where the court made clear that its reasoning in *Connors* was not 'confined only to cases involving the eviction of gipsies or cases where the applicant sought to challenge the law itself rather than its application in [a] particular case', ruling that any person at risk of loss of his or her home

> should in principle be able to have the proportionality of the measure determined by an independent tribunal in the light of the relevant principles under article 8 of the Convention, notwithstanding that, under domestic law, his right of occupation has come to an end.[80]

[77] (2004) 40 EHRR 189.
[78] (2008) 47 EHRR 913.
[79] *Harrow London Borough Council* v. *Qazi* [2003] UKHL 43, [2004] 1 AC 983.
[80] *McCann*, n. 78 above, para. 50.

This ruling has been criticised and discounted by the House of Lords,[81] and it can be asserted with some confidence that the result is not one which our domestic courts would have reached, since the House of Lords in a series of cases, initially by a majority, latterly unanimously, rejected it.[82] There is room for more than one view on this issue, as the divisions of opinion in this country make clear. For those, like me, who prefer what is understood to be the Strasbourg approach, its strength lies in its recognition of the paramount importance to some people, however few, in some circumstances, however rare, of their home, even if their right to live in it has under domestic law come to an end.

My fifth and final group of Article 8 cases concerns the intimate and sensitive area of sexual behaviour. The Strasbourg court has found violations by the United Kingdom in its maintenance of a law criminalising homosexual relations between adult males in Northern Ireland,[83] and a similar law criminalising gross indecency between adult males in private.[84] It also condemned the blanket policy of the Ministry of Defence to exclude homosexuals from the armed forces, a policy which had led to distasteful enquiry into individuals' personal propensities and to the discharge of men whose conduct

---

[81] *Doherty* v. *Birmingham City Council (Secretary of State for Communities and Local Government intervening)* [2008] UKHL 57, [2009] 1 AC 367, paras. 20, 82–8.

[82] *Harrow London Borough Council* v. *Qazi*, n. 79 above; *Kay* v. *Lambeth London Borough Council* [2006] UKHL 10, [2006] 2 AC 465; *Doherty* v. *Birmingham City Council*, n. 81 above.

[83] *Dudgeon* v. *United Kingdom* (1981) 4 EHRR 149.

[84] *ADT* v. *United Kingdom* (2001) 31 EHRR 803.

had given no cause for complaint.[85] Claims by transsexuals that their Article 8 rights were violated by the failure of domestic law to recognise their new gender proved more troublesome. The earliest applications to Strasbourg were rejected.[86] But the tide turned in the applicants' favour in 2002 when, in view of the changed approach to gender reassignment in a number of European countries including Britain, the Grand Chamber found a breach of Article 8 in the UK's failure to give it legal recognition.[87]

These were decisions by which the UK, as a party, had undertaken to abide.[88] The same results could of course have been achieved by political action, but it is at least doubtful whether they would have been. Homosexuals and transsexuals are not groups commanding widespread public or parliamentary support; there was a widespread if historically unsound belief that homosexuals were likely to be effeminate and so unsuitable warriors; and when the ban on 'gays in the military' was challenged in the English courts, before the Convention was given domestic effect, the challenge failed,[89] even though Simon Brown LJ presciently opined that, so far as the

[85] *Lustig-Prean* v. *United Kingdom* (1999) 29 EHRR 449; *Perkins and R* v. *United Kingdom*, judgment of 22 October 2002; *Smith and Grady* v. *United Kingdom* (2000) 29 EHRR 493; *Beck, Copp and Bazeley* v. *United Kingdom*, judgment of 22 October 2002.

[86] *Rees* v. *United Kingdom* (1986) 9 EHRR 56; *Cossey* v. *United Kingdom* (1990) 13 EHRR 622; *X, Y and Z* v. *United Kingdom* (1997) 24 EHRR 143; *Sheffield and Horsham* v. *United Kingdom* (1998) 27 EHRR 163.

[87] *Goodwin* v. *United Kingdom* (2002) 35 EHRR 447; *I* v. *United Kingdom* (2003) 36 EHRR 967; *Grant* v. *United Kingdom* (2007) 44 EHRR 1.

[88] Article 46(1) of the Convention.

[89] *R* v. *Ministry of Defence, Ex p. Smith* [1996] QB 517.

UK's international obligations were concerned, the days of the policy were numbered.[90] These are not, to be sure, decisions which would have been made in 1950 when the Convention was adopted. But they are surely to be welcomed. In a humane society the law should protect the rights of vulnerable minorities as well as dominant majorities, and interpretation of the Convention as a living instrument,[91] responding to the changing needs of society, serves to promote that end.

For reasons of time and space this examination has been confined to a brief survey of cases decided under Article 8. It shows, I suggest, that our law has been enriched by the injection of international jurisprudence, emanating from Strasbourg, and binding on the UK in international law. It has been recently and cogently argued by Lord Hoffmann that human rights should be universal in abstraction but national in application.[92] He fortifies his argument by criticism of three Strasbourg decisions, chosen out of many, two adverse to the UK under Article 6 and one (ultimately favourable to the UK) under Article 8.[93] He would, as I understand, envisage that national courts could draw on the decisions of foreign courts if they chose but would be free to apply the universal human rights principles to their own national situations as they judged appropriate.

This is an alternative model, which no doubt appeals to some, and might well have appealed to Miss Hamlyn. It

---

[90] *Ibid.* at 542.
[91] *Tyrer* v. *United Kingdom* (1978) 2 EHRR 1, para. 16.
[92] 'The Universality of Human Rights', *Law Quarterly Review* 125 (2009) 416–32 at 422.
[93] *Ibid.* at t 424–7.

would not have appealed to Jeremy Bentham, whose famous dismissal of human rights as 'nonsense on stilts'[94] would no doubt have been even more withering had what he regarded as nonsense been on international stilts. And of course there are decisions made by the Strasbourg court, as by any other court, with which we may disagree. But national application, beyond the margin of national appreciation for which the Convention allows, must inevitably lead to significantly differential application between state and state. Lost would be the ideal, boldly proclaimed in 1948, imperfectly realised but noble in conception, that there are some rights so basic that they should be enjoyed by everyone everywhere. I leave the last word to that great sage Amartya Sen:

> Even though contemporary attacks on intellectual globalisation tend to come not only from traditional isolationists but also from modern separatists, we have to recognize that our global civilization is a world heritage – not just a collection of disparate local cultures.[95]

[94] 'Anarchical Fallacies' (1792), republished in *The Works of Jeremy Bentham*, ed. J. Bowring, vol. II (Edinburgh: William Tait, 1843), 501.

[95] 'The Diaspora and the World' in *The Argumentative Indian* (Harmondsworth: Penguin Books, 2006), 85.

'abroad', Lord Hailsham's attitude
    to 1
access to court, ECHR Article 6
    right of 45
accusation of adultery, fear of 38–9
advocate's immunity to claims
    of negligence in court
    proceedings, claims against
    11–13
Al-Jedda v. *Secretary of State for
    Defence* 49–54
Amartya Sen, comments on global
    civilisation 83
American Declaration of the Rights
    and Duties of Man 1948,
    adoption of 56
'anathema', international
    Conventions as 31–2
asbestos claims 13–16

Barbados, human rights challenge
    to mandatory death
    sentence 68–9
Behrami v. *France* 51–4
Belize, human rights challenge to
    mandatory death sentence
    65–7
Bentham, Jeremy, view on human
    rights 83
Bermuda, human rights law 59–60

Bill of Rights 1791 (US),
    extra-territoriality of 55
Bingham of Cornhill, Lord
    interpretation of Hague
    Convention on Child
    Abduction, view on 40
    opinion 52
    respect for prisoners' rights, on
    78–80
Boyce v. *Barbados* 68–9
Brightman of Ibthorpe, Lord,
    prolonged-delay death
    sentence, on 61
British law
    Miss Hamlyn's belief in
    25–8
    use by foreign jurisdictions
    25–8
Brown LJ, Simon, view on armed
    forces ban on homosexuals
    81
Brown of Eaton-under-Heywood,
    Lord, opinion 52
Browne-Wilkinson of Camden,
    Lord, view on interpretation
    of international conventions
    33
Byron CJ, Sir Denis, mandatory
    death sentence judgment
    64–5

Canary Wharf Tower, interference
with television reception
20–1
Canivet, Conseiller Guy, support
for use of comparative
law 7
Caribbean Court of Justice,
establishment of 63–4
Carriage of Goods by Sea Act 1924,
opposition to 31–2
Carswell, Lord, opinion 52
Cazalet, Mr Justice Edward, use of
foreign authorities 24–5
chain of causation, mesothelioma
claims 13–16
child abduction, Hague Convention
33–7
Child Abduction and Custody Act
1985 33–7
City of London, use of foreign
attachment procedure
25–8
Clyde, Lord, use of foreign
authorities 22
comparative law *see also* foreign
authorities
impoverishment of law through
ignorance of 6
mission 4–5
objections to 3–4
problems with ignoring 5–6
support for use of 6–7
use of 3–28
concurrent claim in tort and
contract 16–17
conflict of laws, sovereign
immunity 45–9

Connors v. *UK* 79
contract damages rule, foreign
origins 5–6
contract law
concurrent claim in tort and
contract 16–17
solicitor's duty in 17–20
use of foreign authorities as to
solicitor's duty 18–20
Council of the European Union,
joint position on refugee
status 42

damages, foreign origins of contract
damages rule 5–6
death sentence
five-year time limit for carrying
out 63–4
mandatory 64–9
prolonged delay 60–4
Declaration of the Rights of Man
and the Citizen 1789
(France), extra-territoriality
of 55
Denning MR, Lord
support for use of foreign
authorities 25–8
view on human rights 55
detention of terrorism suspect
49–54
Devlin, Lord
Hague Rules, view on
interpretation of 32–3
human rights law, view on 58
DPP v. *Nasralla* 58
Drittschadensliquidation, use of
18–20

European Convention on Human
Rights 1951
  adoption 56
  Article 5, right of personal
    freedom 49–54
  Article 6
    right of access to court 45
    torture claims 48–9
  Article 8 violations by UK 71–2
  British courts, in 70–83
  extension to UK overseas
    territories 56–7
  Privy Council application of
    57–70
  ex-colonial constitutions, human
    rights law in 57–70

Fairchild v. Glenhaven Funeral
  Services 13–16
female genital mutilation, fear of
  39–40
foreign attachment procedure, use
  in City of London 25–8
foreign authorities
  historic use of 5–6
  situations where influential
    7–8
  use where domestic authority
    gives inappropriate or
    unjust answer 8–16
  no clear answer 16–25
'foreign moods, fads, or fashions',
  Justice Scalia's objections
    to 4
foreign states, UK court jurisdiction
  in 44–9
Fox v. The Queen 64–5

Geneva Convention relating to the
  Status of Refugees 1951
  definition of 'refugee' 38
  interpretation of 37–44
  purpose 38
Goff of Chieveley, Lord
  support for use of comparative
    law 6–7
  use of foreign authorities 9–10,
    16–17, 18–21
Greatorex v. Greatorex 23–5
Griffiths, Lord, judgment on
  prolonged delay in death
    sentence 62–3

Hadley v. Baxendale rule, foreign
  origins 5–6
Hague Convention on the Civil
  Aspects of International
  Child Abduction
  interpretation of 33–7
  motivating principle 34
  objects 34
  wrongful removal or retention of
    child 34
Hague Rules (carriage of goods by
  sea), domestic authority
    31–2
Hailsham, Lord, attitude to
  'abroad' 1
Hale of Richmond, Lady, opinion 52
Hall & Co. v. Simons 11–13
Hamlyn, Miss Emma Warburton
  belief in British law 1
  knowledge of law 1–2
  legacy vi–vii, 1
  life vi

Hamlyn Lectures
  61st series viii–ix, 3
  content of current series 3, 29
  origins 1
Hamlyn Trust
  objects vii–viii
  overview vi–viii
  trustees vii
Harding, Professor Andrew,
    view on Privy Council's
    experience of human rights
    law 57–8
Henderson v. *Merrett Syndicates*
  16–17
Hoffman, Lord
  application of ECHR, view
    on 82
  precedence of torture
    prohibition, view on 45–6
  Reyes v. *The Queen*, comments
    on 67
Hope of Craighead, Lord, use of
    foreign authorities 22–3
Human Rights Act 1998 (HRA)
  effect of 45, 49
  exception to State Immunity Act
    1978 48–9
  impact 70–1
human rights law
  British courts, in 55–83
  ex-colonial constitutions, in
    57–70
  Miss Hamlyn's understanding
    of 55–6
  pre-UDHR 55–6
Hunter v. *Canary Wharf Ltd*
  20–1

immunity *see* sovereign immunity
inappropriate result, use of foreign
    authorities where otherwise
    8–16
inhuman or degrading treatment or
    punishment
  human rights challenge
    64–5
  mandatory death sentence as
    64–9
  prolonged delay in carrying out
    death sentence as 60–4
  UN Convention against 46–9
interception of private
    communications, ECHR
    Article 8 violations 72–4
international law
  'anathema', as 31–2
  British courts, in 29–54
  declaration by Lord Mansfield
    30–1
  domestic authority conferred by
    statute 31–7
  domestic authority without
    statute 37–44
  increased role 29–30
  meaning 30–1
  practice areas where arising 30
Iraq, British courts' jurisdiction
    over detainees held in 51–4

Jamaica
  death sentence, prolonged delay
    60–4
  human rights law 58
Jones v. *Saudi Arabia Interior
    Ministry* 44–9

judge's task 1–2
jurisdiction, British
    British courts in foreign states
        44–9
    detainees held in Iraq 49–54

KFOR action, UN liability for 51–4
Kleinwort Benson v. *Lincoln City
    Council* 8–10
Kosovo, UN liability for operations
    in 51–4

Lauterpacht, Professor Sir Hersch,
    views on UDHR 56
Lloyd's disputes 16–17

Magna Carta 1215, extra-
    territoriality of 55
Malawi, human rights challenge to
    mandatory death sentence
    67–8
Mansfield, Lord, view on
    international law 31
McCann v. *UK* 79–80
McFarlane v. *Tayside Health Board*
    21–3
medical negligence, claims 21–3
mesothelioma claims 13–16
Millett, Lord, use of foreign
    authorities 22–3
Minister of Home Affairs v. *Fisher*
    59–60
mistake of law, recovery of money
    paid under 8–10

negligence
    court proceedings, claims against
        advocate's immunity in 11–13

extent of solicitor's duty of care
    17–20
medical negligence 21–3
self-inflicted injuries, victim's
    duty to third parties 23–5
solicitor, by 11–13, 17–20
no clear answer, use of foreign
    authorities where otherwise
    16–25
'nonsense on stilts', human rights
    law as 83

overseas territories, ECHR
    extended to 56–7

persecution, fear of
    membership of particular social
        group, for 37–44
    non-state agents, by 40–1
    one part of home country, in
        41–4
personal data, access to, ECHR
    Article 8 violations 74–6
Petition of Rights 1628, extra-
    territoriality 55
Pratt v. *A-G of Jamaica* 62–4
prisoners' correspondence,
    ECHR Article 8 violations
    76–8
private nuisance claims 20–1
Privy Council, application of
    human rights law 57–70
psychiatric injury to third party,
    duty not to cause 23–5

R v. *Hughes* 65
recovery of money paid under
    mistake of law 8–10

'refugee', Geneva Convention
    definition of 38
refugee status
    fear of persecution, due to
        see persecution, fear of
    Geneva Convention,
        interpretation of 37–44
    guidance 42
    respect for the home, ECHR
        Article 8 violations
        78–80
Reyes v. The Queen 65–7
Rhodesia and Nyasaland, human
    rights challenge to
    mandatory death sentence
    67
'rights attributed to a person',
    Hague Convention on Child
    Abduction, interpretation
    of 35–6
'rights of custody', Hague
    Convention on Child
    Abduction, interpretation
    of 35–6
Riley v. A-G of Jamaica 60–2
Rodger of Earlsferry, Lord, opinion
    49–54
Rondel v. Worsley 11–13
Roskill, Lord, view on opposition
    to Carriage of Goods by Sea
    Act 1924 32–3

saisie conservatoire, use of 25–8
Saramati v. France, Germany and
    Norway 51–4
Scalia, Justice Antonin, objections
    to use of foreign
    authorities 4

Scarman, Lord, view on prolonged
    delay in carrying out death
    sentence 61
Schutzwirkung für Dritte, use of
    18–20
seizure of goods under City of
    London foreign attachment
    procedure 25–8
self-inflicted injuries, victim's duty
    to third party 23–5
sexual behaviour, freedom of,
    ECHR Article 8 violations
    80–2
Slynn of Hadley, Lord, use of
    foreign authorities 22–3
Soering v. United Kingdom 63
solicitor, negligence claim against
    17–20
sovereign immunity
    law of 44–9
    UN Convention on Immunity 48
St Christopher and Nevis, human
    rights challenge to
    mandatory death sentence
    64–5
St Lucia, human rights challenge to
    mandatory death sentence
    64–5
St Vincent, human rights challenge
    to mandatory death
    sentence 64–5
State Immunity Act 1978
    HRA exception to 48–9
    UK court jurisdiction in foreign
        states under 44
statute, conferral of domestic
    authority of international
    law by 31–7

Steyn, Lord
  Hague Rules, comment on 32–3
  use of foreign authorities 11–13,
    22–3

television reception, interference
    with 20–1
terrorism, detention of suspect
    49–54
time limit for carrying out death
    sentence 63–4
tort law
  concurrent claim in tort and
    contract 16–17
  solicitor's duty in 17–20
  use of foreign authorities in
    asbestos claims 14–15
torture
  claims 44–9
  precedence of prohibition of
    45–6
  UN Convention 46–9
Trinidad and Tobago, human rights
    challenge to mandatory
    death sentence 68–9
trustees, Hamlyn Trust vii
Tyrer v. United Kingdom 61

Uganda, human rights challenge to
    mandatory death sentence
    68
UN Convention on Immunity,
    torture claims under 48
UN Security Council resolutions,
    precedence of 49–54

United Nations, liability for
    operations in Kosovo 51–4
United Nations Convention against
    Torture and other Cruel,
    Inhuman or Degrading
    Treatment or Punishment,
    civil claims under 46–9
United Nations Convention on
    Jurisdictional Immunities of
    States and Their Property 45
United Nations High
    Commissioner for Refugees
    (UNHCR), guidance 42
Universal Declaration of Human
    Rights 1948 (UDHR)
  human rights law prior to 55–6
  importance 56
unjust decision, use of foreign
    authorities where otherwise
    8–16
UNMIK action, UN liability for
    51–4
unwanted pregnancy and
    childbirth, negligence claim
    21–3

Vienna Convention on the Law of
    Treaties 1980, invocation 40
Visby Protocol 1968, conferral
    of domestic authority by
    statute 32–3

White v. Jones 17–20
Wilberforce, Lord, view on human
    rights law 59–60